A History Of Life On Earth

Bruce Alpine

A History Of Life On Earth

Bruce Alpine

Copyright © 2012 by Bruce H. Alpine

queries@brucealpine.com

Book Layout ©2016 Bruce H. Alpine

A History Of Life On Earth

ePub ISBN: 978-1-301-20346-8
Print ISBN: 978-1-493-53927-7

About The Author

B ruce Alpine is a science writer based out of the Kapiti Coast in New Zealand. Renowned for his ability to explain complex and technical issues in a way that is both easy to understand and fun to read, Bruce has gained a small but devoted audience since he published his first book, A History Of Life On Earth.

Born in Wellington, New Zealand in 1958, Bruce was the only son of a former college instructor. His mother was born in Britain and immigrated to New Zealand when she was 21. She encouraged Bruce and his three sisters to read often and study hard in school, and when it became clear that Bruce had an affinity for science, she encouraged that too.

Bruce's key interests revolve around the Earth and the life that inhabits it: how it sprang up, how it's come to be the way it is, how it functions now, etc. In addition to his work as a writer, Bruce is employed in the health support industry. He has two children, one son and one daughter, both of whom are grown up.

Contact The Author:
Bruce-a@brucealpine.com

Discover More Titles From Bruce Alpine:
https://brucealpine.com

Contents

Learn from yesterday, live for today, hope for tomorrow. The most important thing is not to stop questioning.

—Albert Einstein

CHAPTER ONE

Origins

A book with a title such as "History Of Life On Earth" must start with the origin of Earth.

The origin of Earth can only start with the origin of the Universe in which the solar system and Earth resides, from which everything originates, including any form of life.

If it were not for the origin of the universe and the solar system, life wouldn't be possible on Earth.

Section 1. **Origins Of The Universe**

1. Introduction.

Imagine not knowing anything about the planet we all know as Earth. Except for your immediate environment you relate to as home.

Imagine that you don't know anything about the mechanics or the workings of the Solar System, and absolutely nothing about the greater Universe.

You may notice the weather changes along with any temperature changes and fluctuations throughout the year. At times the temperature is warmer than at other times. At times, some wet substance is falling from the sky. Other times something in the sky is shining and feels warmer, shining on you. When this shiny thing is visible, the sky is blue; at other times it is black in appearance and other phenomena are occurring as well. Little lights are flickering and seem stationary.

Imagine lying down on the ground and looking at those little lights for the first time. You may notice they are slowly revolving around the sky. It seems strange because while the sky was blue, that strange light in the sky seemed to make everything brighter. Now there is another object replacing it; round, grey and not as bright as the previous object. At times, this round thing is in the shape of a crescent. At other times it is fully rounded. You can see it because it is also light - although, not as bright as the other object.

After a short while, you may notice all these things seem to happen in some cycle. The only problem is that you don't know why and how. You may start to imagine some higher power or, intelligent designer, controlling it. You may even imagine, all this was created by that imaginary being. After a short while, the only viable explanation is this mythical Creator.

This book is based on scientific evidence, evidence that has been tested and proved many times. It all began as a hypothesis.

That hypothesis was tested and proved to be true. It progressed to a theory.

2.Scientific Hypotheses and Scientific Theory

To begin with, I feel it is notable to point out a couple of terms that are commonly used with science, including common misconceptions or misinterpretations that relate to those terms.

The terms I am referring to are: scientific hypothesis and scientific theory. The two words: hypothesis and theory, when used in science, differ from the usual definitions and commonly lead to confusion.

The common scientific definition of the terms, leads to misconceptions by the general public. Scientific hypothesis and scientific theory tend to be regarded as mere guesses; not proved and may even lack credibility. In scientific terms scientific hypothesis is an educated guess considering observations; a rational explanation for what has been physically observed, but has not been proved. Most scientific hypotheses can be proved through further observations and experimentations thus becoming a scientific theory.

Scientific Theory: Once the hypothesis has been proved through continued observations and experimentation, it is verified and accepted to be true. At this point it becomes a scientific theory.

A scientific theory can then be tested by multiple groups of scientists, with different methods of experimentation and observations. These are then verified and accepted by a wider scientific community to be true; known as peer review. A, scientific theory is generally accepted by the scientific community to be, fact. So, when scientists are referring to a theory such as the Big Bang theory or the theory of Evolution they are stating them as fact.

2. In The Beginning.

Prior to 13.7 billion years ago, there was nothing, not even time, until a phenomena known as the Big Bang occurred, which created the Universe. British theoretical physicist and cosmologist, Stephen Hawking best describes the event as part of the, "Big Fizz Theory of Origins".

Theorists are beginning to believe the 'Big Bang' could be better described as part of the 'Big Bounce'; believing the Universe may have existed previously, but collapsed in on itself, before expanding into the Universe we know today.

That is how it is with science. Once an origin is established, a new theory will evolve, questioning the origins of the origin. In other words, for an event such as the 'Big Bang' something must have happened before the event. The 'Big Fizz' theory of origins and the 'Big Bounce' theory revolve around the idea that a previous Universe existed before this Universe. The previous Universe may have contracted and formed that infinitely dense mass, forcing a re-expansion that would become today's Universe. Our Universe may have, 'Bounced' into existence.

This contraction and re-expansion may be cyclical and have caused an infinite succession of, 'Bangs' and 'Bounces', in the past.

3. The "Big Bang"

The Big Bang is not a Theory at all. It is a model or a scenario, for which there is overwhelming evidence. The Big Bang, as a theory originated in 1922, by a Belgian Roman Catholic priest and scientist, Monsignor Georges Lemaître, who called the theory, 'The Big Noise' while describing the event as, "A primeval atom, exploding at the moment of creation as the "Day Without Yesterday."

"The Big Bang," as a phrase, was coined by the English astronomer and mathematician Fred Hoyle in 1949, as a pejorative. Because he disagreed with the interpretation of the theory. Hoyle argued: instead, for the Universe being in a steady state. This was later disproved by the American astronomer, Edwin Hubble.

Hubble was able to determine that the Universe was expanding. So it was not steady. Modern scientists believe this best describes this singular event, so, it has therefore been adopted by the scientific community. The Big Bang is a well tested theory, accepted by the scientific community, as the most accurate and comprehensive explanation of the origins of the Universe, including all the phenomena astronomers observe today.

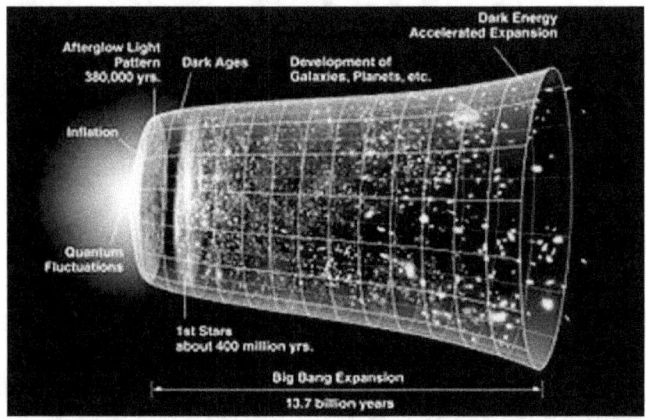

An artist's impression of the Universe expansion. Where space is represented at each time by the circular sections.

Discoveries in astronomy and physics have shown beyond any reasonable doubt, that the Universe does have a beginning. Before that, there was nothing. After that, there was an ever-expanding Universe. The Big Bang explains, what happened during and after, in a singular event that was the origin of the Universe and, everything.

4. Misconception.

Many people hold a misconception that the Big Bang describes the beginning of the Universe. As a theory the Big Bang explanation stays quiet of the actual origins of the Universe. It assumes the energy that caused the sudden, massive expansion already existed. The Big Bang tells us nothing of why the Universe was born hot and dense to begin with, as the physical laws do not yet apply to such extremes in nature.

Another major, common misconception relating to the Big Bang is that people tend to imagine an enormous explosion, which suddenly happened. Suddenly everything appeared, as if a gigantic balloon popped and released everything. This is not so, as scientists believe the event to be a sudden expansion, instead of an explosion. You could still use the example of a balloon, but only by imagining a very small balloon containing a very small, compact, extremely hot, blob of soup, with an extreme density - then suddenly expanding to the size of today's Universe. That balloon contained everything that is now known as the Universe.

The singular event of the Big Bang is a point of extremely high temperature and infinite density; the same conditions that exist inside a Black Hole today. Black Holes are areas of intense gravitational pressure. The pressure is thought to be so intense, that finite matter is squished into infinite density. As a mathematical idea this is quite mind boggling.

These zones of infinite density are called, singularities. This singularity is of soup, floated in a vacuum until it expanded with gas and energy ejecting in all directions at high speed to become the Universe.

6. Evolution Of The Universe

The evolution of the Universe and all we know about the Universe, and the planet we consider to be home, began with this singular event of an extremely hot and dense state, which expanded rapidly, creating the young Universe. Matter and antimatter collided. In the process destroying each other and creating light. There was however more matter than antimatter. When this natural process was over, there remained matter and a tremendous amount of light.

For three hundred thousand years after the Big Bang, the Universe was filled with radiation and minute particles. The growing Universe was intensely hot after this rapid expansion and eventual cooling. Various physical forces allowed energy to convert to subatomic particles.

After some 380 thousand years, some of these particles, consisting of quarks, leptons, protons, neutrons and electrons would combine and form atoms. The initial elements this process produced, were hydrogen as well as traces of helium and lithium.

As the gas formed, it expanded and under gravity, formed great clouds of matter. These clouds formed into massive clusters with enormous empty spaces between. Gradually, under gravity, galaxies coalesced, forming groups within the clusters. This recombination dramatically changed the growing Universe. Eventually after another billion years, clouds of hydrogen would coalesce through gravity and form stars. The heavier elements would synthesize within stars or supernova. Stars have continued to form and light the Universe ever since.

In July 2012, scientists at the CERN in Switzerland observed the hypothetical particle known as the Higgs Boson or God Particle. It is general knowledge in the scientific community that any particles that make up mass are bound together by either gravity, electron or colour charges. According to quantum physics, this principle is the same, however, when an atomic particle is so small, as it is with a subatomic particle, gravity has no effect on the particles. Therefore something must be binding these particles together. In 1964, British physicist, Peter Higgs proposed a theoretical Particle or Boson which if true is responsible for the binding of such atoms, giving them mass. So the theoretical particle as proposed by Higgs gained the name "Higgs Boson" or in popular culture "God Particle."

Technically it is the Higgs Boson that gives mass to the elementary particles, such as Quarks and Electrons. Previous to July 2012, this Boson had not been observed. This discovery or observation shines enlightenment upon how the elementary subatomic particle attracted and formed mass in the early Universe.

About nine billion years after the Big Bang, an unusually dense swirl of dust formed our Solar System. One of the spiral arms of the Milky Way collapsed under the weight of gravity. Ninety-nine point nine percent of the swirl became our sun. The other one percent went into the planets or became other objects in the sun's orbit.

According to Albert Einstein, space is not simply emptiness. It stretches and is flexible. Einstein's Theory of Gravity, suggests the Universe is expanding and describes a relationship between space, time and matter. Astronomer, Edwin Hubble in the 1920s, observed that distant galaxies are drifting away from each other just as Einstein suggested and as would be expected after a Big Bang or a sudden massive expansion event. Einstein's theory of General Relativity, predicted that the Universe must either be expanding or contracting.

Using Einstein's Theory of Relativity, scientists can determine how fast the Universe has been expanding in the past. Using that information they can turn back the clock and determine when the Universe was zero size. According to Einstein, the time between then and now, determines the age of the Universe.

In 1924, Edwin Hubble was able to determine that the Universe was expanding. He observed galaxies and stars drifting away from each other and our Solar System. He was able to do this by using the Doppler Effect.

The Doppler Effect was proposed in 1842, by an Austrian physicist, Christian Doppler, using sound waves to determine the distance between objects. When an object is close, the sound waves returning are compacted or closer together. When an object is farther apart, the sound waves are less compact or further apart. When objects are moving farther apart, the sound waves give a different frequency.

The same effect can be experienced when an ambulance, siren blaring, is moving towards you. You get each wave travelling a shorter distance. When the ambulance has passed, the sound waves travel an increasingly greater distance as the ambulance travels further away. Or, the received frequency is higher, compared to the emitted frequency during the approach. It is identical at the instant of passing by. It is progressively lower during the recession.

For waves, which do not require a medium, such as light or gravity, in general relativity, only the relative difference in velocity between observer and source needs to be considered. Hubble was able to show that the velocity of a distant galaxy, measured from Earth, was directly proportional to the distance of the galaxy from Earth. He expressed the direct proportion between velocity and distance as: $v=Hd$, which, became known as 'Hubble's Constant'- Constant being the constant expansion of today's Universe.

Hubble's Constant has been important in determining the age of the Universe. Hubble's findings also proved that the Big Bang theory might be right.

Using Einstein's General Relativity and Hubble's Constant, NASA's Wilkinson Microwave Anisotropy Probe (WMAP) project estimated the age of the universe to be: 13.7 billion years.

The WMAP is a co-venture by NASA, Goddard Space Flight Centre and Princeton University named after cosmologist, David Wilkinson (1935– 2002). A space

craft measures the remnant radiant heat from the Big
Bang, across the Universe.

Today, the Universe continues to cool and expand. We are part of
it. It is all around us; Earth sits amongst it. The Hubble ultra-deep
field highlights galaxies from an earlier era when the Universe was
younger, denser, and warmer according to the Big Bang theory.

Section 2. **Evolution**

1. Introduction

Evolution is any change in the heritable characteristics
of biological populations across successive generations,
leading to diversity in every level of biological organisation. It includes species, individual organisms, DNA
and protein molecules, using both existing species and
the fossil record. Evolution is the study of universal
common ancestors' origin on Earth 3.7 billion years
ago that leads to an explanation of all life on Earth.
Another common misconception is that Charles Darwin
first proposed evolution. This is a fallacy.

- As far back as 611-547 B.C., ancient Greek philosopher, Anaxiamander hypothesized that:

"In the beginning there was a fishlike creature with scales that arose in and lived in the world oceans. As some of these advanced, they moved onto land, shed their scaly coverings and became the first humans."

- The Roman philosopher Lucretius (99-55 B.C.) was the first to realise that all living things were related and that they had changed over time. In his book, De Rerum Natura (On the Nature of Things), Lucretius wrote:

"Wherefore, again, again, how merited is that adopted name of Earth -the Mother!

Since she herself begat the human race; and at one well-nigh fixed time brought forth each breast that ranges raving round about upon the mighty mountains and all birds aerial with many a varied shape.

But, lo, because her bearing years must end, she ceased, like to a woman worn by eld.

For lapsing aeons change the nature of the whole wide world, and all things needs must take one status after other, nor aught persists forever like itself.

All things depart; Nature she changeth all, compelleth all to transformation."

- Aristotle, (384 BC – 322 BC) developed his Scala Naturae, or Ladder of Life to explain his idea of the advancement of living things, from inanimate matter to plants. Then animals and finally man.

- Georges-Louis Leclerc, Comte de Buffon in the middle to late 1700s proposed that species could change.

- Erasmus Darwin, A British physician and poet in the late 1700s, proposed that life had changed over time. His poem titled, Origin of Society. Includes:

"Hence without parent by spontaneous birth
Rise the first specks of animated Earth; From
Nature's womb the plant or insect swims,
And buds or breathes, with microscopic limbs.

ORGANIC LIFE beneath the shoreless waves
Was born and nurs'd in Ocean's pearly caves.
First forms minute, unseen by spheric glass,
Move on the mud, or pierce the watery mass;
These, as successive generations bloom.

New powers acquire, and larger limbs assume;
Whence countless groups of vegetation spring,
And breathing realms of fin, and feet, and wing."

- William Smith (1769-1839), developed the Principle of Biological Succession by stating:

"Each period of Earth history, has its own unique assemblages of fossils."

- Jean Baptiste de Lamarck, developed one of the first theories on how species changed. Lamarck, in 1809, concluded that organisms of higher complexity had evolved from pre-existing, less complex organisms.

2 Evolution And Charles Darwin.

It is not a mere coincidence that Erasmus Darwin, shares the same surname as Charles Darwin. Erasmus Darwin was Charles Darwin's grandfather and certainly influenced Charles's thinking, probably throughout his entire life; certainly after Charles's five-year expedition onboard the survey ship *HMS Beagle*, during the 1830s.

Charles Darwin certainly was not the first to realise that species diversify and change over time. He was however, the first to collect enough evidence and so formulating his theory on evolution, through his book, *Origin Of Species. - By Means of Natural Selection.*

Darwin was born in Shropshire England in 1809.

Initially, he chose to follow a medical career, at Edinburgh, later changing to divinity at Cambridge. In 1831, Darwin was convinced by Professor Henslow at Cambridge, to join the scientific survey ship, *Beagle*, taking in the Southern Oceans, the South American coast and Australia with Captain Robert Fitzroy.

In 1842, Charles Darwin penned an early version of his Theory of Evolution, which would become his book, on the *"Origin Of Species, By Means Of Natural Selection.'*

During the voyage, Darwin read Lyell's, '*Principles of Geology*', which suggested that the fossils found in rocks were evidence of animals that had lived many thousands or millions of years ago. During his voyage, Lyell's ideas were reinforced in Darwin's mind. While he visited the Galapagos Islands, Darwin realised the diversity of finches between the islands that were closely related but different in important ways. For example, travelling from island to island, Darwin noticed that finch populations inhabiting islands that mainly provided nuts had thicker, larger beaks. On islands, that mainly provided berries, finch populations had smaller, narrower beaks. The geographical isolation between the islands caused finch populations to diversify and adapt to their different environments.

On his return to England in 1836, Darwin immediately set to work and produced his book, "*Zoology Of The Beagle.*"

In 1841, Darwin was also becoming increasingly curious about his findings. He worked on his theory of Evolution, by natural selection, for twenty years. He derived his theory of Natural Selection after reading papers from Thomas Malthus.

Malthus proposed a theory of evolution occurring by the process of natural selection. Animals and plants are much more likely to reproduce with characteristics in their offspring best suited to their environment. The species change gradually over time. After learning about similar findings from Alfred Wallace, another naturalist, in 1858, Darwin was persuaded to publish his book in 1859.

Upon publication, Darwin's - *Origin of species: By Means Of Natural Selection*, sold out within a day and received raving reviews, since publication, including from Sir Julian Huxley, who wrote:

"*is the most powerful and the most comprehensive idea that has ever arisen on Earth. It helps us understand our origins ... We are part of a total process, made of the same matter and operating by the same energy as the rest of the cosmos, maintaining and reproducing by the same type of mechanism as the rest of life."*

Julian Huxley was an English evolutionary biologist; the first director of UNESCO and a founding member of World Wildlife Fund, WWF.

Darwin's theory of evolution, by means of natural selection is no longer a theory. An overwhelming amount of evidence has been collected since Darwin's time, to the extent that no argument since has successfully refuted Darwin's claims. *'Origin Of Species, By Means Of Natural Selection'*, has become the standard explanation for life on Earth, from its origins to modern times.

Charles Darwin died on April 19, 1882. He was honoured in June, 1909, by more than four hundred officials and scientists who met in Cambridge, to commemorate the fiftieth anniversary of the publication of *On The Origins Of Species*, and of Darwin's one-hundredth Birthday.

3. Misconceptions

A misconception of Darwin's theory is that some groups believe that in *'Origin Of Species, by Means Of Natural Selection'*, Darwin claims that humans evolved from apes. Darwin does not mention humans in *'Origin Of Species'*, except for one little passage in the last chapter, third paragraph from the end. Darwin writes:

"In the distant future, light will be thrown on the origin of man and his history."

Humans and apes did share a common ancestor five to eight million years ago. Shortly thereafter, the species diverged into two separate lineages. One of these ultimately evolved into gorillas and chimps. The other evolved into early human ancestors called Hominids. Genetically, humans are still ninety-nine percent chimpanzee.

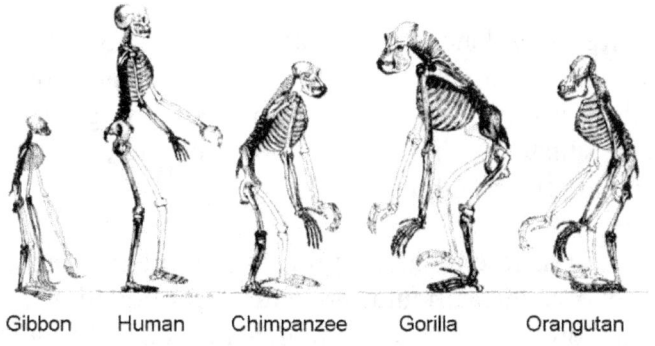

Gibbon   Human   Chimpanzee   Gorilla   Orangutan

Hominids are descended from common ancestors.

It was claimed that Darwin renounced his theory of evolution, on his deathbed. Evangelist and temperance campaigner, Lady Elizabeth Hope, claimed she visited Darwin at his deathbed, and witnessed the renunciation. Later her claim was printed in a Boston newspaper. Darwin's daughter, Henrietta refuted Lady Hope's claim by stating:

"I was present at his deathbed. He never recanted any of his scientific views, either then or earlier."

5. Evidence Supports Evolution

The Science behind evolution is constant and continually advancing. New discoveries are made almost daily. These advances are through discoveries of new fossils that support the evolution theory. Fossils cannot be altered or changed in any way, they are a record in time: from the first living organisms, through diversification or adaptation, through different environments, to the more complex and advanced species occupying Earth today.

The fossil evidence for evolution clearly shows lineage from ancestor to ancestor, through eon to eon, from geological period to geological period, throughout Earth's history. They clearly show that life cannot originate from nothing.

Through different natural processes, genes will emerge and evolve throughout time in different mutations, passed on from generation to generation. The genes not passed on, are those proving somewhat incompatible to the processional method that should benefit the following generations. Thus is the concept of natural selection.

Some confusion around evolution is the notion that evolutionary changes can occur within a generation. This is a fallacy as any changes within a generation is a mutation.

Mutations are not a genetic change, so will not be passed onto following generations.

Therefore, the Selfish Gene. The idea of the selfish gene infers, the gene is selfish, not the individual possessing that gene. Sceptics of evolution, infer there should be a missing link. Evolutionary evidence clearly shows the lineages of species occurring over thousands and millions of years. A single generation will not notice any changes however over multiple generations many minute changes will be noticed.

Fossil evidence is a snapshot in time. Evolutionary changes, within species are evident in the fossil record. Evolutionary changes will not appear within a single sedimentary layer but over various sedimentary layers the evidence is clear. In short. Evolution refers to a change in the gene pool of a population, not of any individual. Failure to adapt, can and will lead to a species extinction.

Humans belong to the group known as Hominid, belonging to the Homo genus. Modern humans belong to the Homo Sapiens evolving from Homo Erectus; progressing to Homo Habilis, genus; deriving from, Ardipithecus species which is believed to have evolved into the, Australopithecus, or Ape Man.

The most recent species of the Ardipithecus species, discovered was the four million years old partial skeletal remains of the Ardipithecus Ramidus. Which was discovered in 1994.

In 2006, a four million year old fossil was discovered in the Middle Awash region of North-Eastern Ethiopia. In this region seven other human-like species, had previously been discovered spanning nearly six million years. They included three major phases of human development. The Middle Awash, is a density of rock which is about a mile thick. Ethiopian anthropologist Berhane Asfaw said, upon the discovery: *"We just found the chain of evolution, the continuity through time."*

The discovery was the link that enabled scientists to complete the chain of human evolution from Ardipithecus to Australopithecus, enabling scientists to see all three phases of human evolution; linking Ardipithecus and Australopithecus as two different species of early humans.

The sedimentary layers containing fossils are a treasure trove for scientists. They confirm that life on Earth has progressed and changed over the past four billion years.

Today scientists may take fossils for granted but they continue to learn from them and continue to provide evidence supporting Charles Darwin's, *Origin of Species, By way of Natural Selection.*

6.   Science Verses Pseudo-Science

The term, science derives from the Latin word for knowledge - Scientia. Therefore pseudo-science, derived again from Latin pseudo = false means, false knowledge.

Science should never be confused with falsehoods. Real science concerns itself with what is visually observed and can be tested by experiment. Only through experimentation, can a hypotheses be proved. Only when a hypotheses is proved, can a theory emerge. If a scientific hypotheses or theory is proved to be incorrect it will be rejected by the wider scientific community.

Pseudo-science concerns itself with what cannot be observed and cannot be tested by experiment. Pseudo-science cannot generate any new predictions and no new hypotheses will emerge. Pseudo-science is usually based on cultural, religious or social beliefs. Such beliefs, if based on mythology, cannot be regarded as science because they are rooted in the supernatural. They may be dependent on an intelligent designer or creator. Science should never be dependent on any preconceived outcome.

CHAPTER TWO

Beginnings

Section 1. **Hadean and Archaean Eons**

So we all know that life on Earth is possible! We are here and so is every other form of life that we know. Three-point five billion years ago, Earth's atmosphere and environment was very different from todays. Modern life would have been impossible. A modern man's chances for survival, even within a short time, would have been extremely bleak.

First, oxygen was scarce so death from suffocation would have been agonising. The other extant chemicals would have been too acidic for human life and most other forms of life sustained on Earth today.

So where did it all come from? What was the starting point?

1. Hadean Eon.

Beginning 4.7 billion years ago with the formation of
Earth, the Hadean Eon, preceded the geological Archaean Eon, ending 3.8 billion years ago. The name
Hadean derives from the Greek word, Hades, meaning,
underworld - referring to the hellish conditions on
Earth at the time of formation, it was coined in 1972 by
geologist, Preston Cloud.

The Solar System was still forming during the Hadean
Eon. The early Earth consisted of molten rock. The
Earth cooled and the molten rock solidified. And thus
began the geological history of the Earth.

    2.   Archaean Eon.

Archaean Eon is the geological period beginning 3.8
billion years ago. It is the period in Earth's history before the Proterozoic Eon. 2.5 billion years ago.

The Earth's heat flow was three times higher than it is
today. The temperature was twice as high as the beginning of the following, Proterozoic Eon. As a result of
the planetary accretion process that formed the Earths
core and produced from Radioactive Elements.

Volcanic Activity was considerably higher at this time,
with numerous lava eruptions. Modern research is centred around, whether Tectonic activity existed during
the Archaean Eon.

Much scientific debate concerns whether the excessive
geological activity created continents during this time.
It questions whether larger continents existed. or,

smaller Proto-continents. Some scientists argue that, because the Earth was much hotter, tectonic activity was more vigorous than it is today. This resulted in a much faster rate of recycling of crustal material. This may have prevented Cratonisation and Continental formation until the mantle cooled and convection slowed down.

Others argue that the Oceanic Lithosphere was too buoyant to subduct; that the rarity of Archaean rock is a function of erosion by subsequent Tectonic events. The debate continues.

Fossils from the Archaean have identified Cyanobacteria or Stromatolites, which are responsible for creating the oxygen levels on Earth creating a base for the evolution of later forms of life.

Respiration instead of fermentation. Stromatolites became particularly common towards the end of the Archaean eon. They limited any life to simple non-nucleated single-celled organisms, called Prokaryote. There are no known Eukaryotic fossils. Though they might have evolved during the Archaean without leaving any fossils. No fossil evidence yet exists for ultra-microscopic intracellular replicators, such as viruses.

Section 2. **Building The Earth**

1. Formation of Earth.

The origins of Earth began about 4.6 billion years ago with a massive, spinning, revolving cloud of dust similar to a revolving disc called a Solar Nebula. The centre of this spinning cloud of gas condensed into a white hot core. After this core reached one million degrees Fahrenheit it ignited through nuclear fusion of hydrogen into helium and became our Sun.

An impression of a Solar nebula, after the sun has ignited. Accretion is building the planets.

Along with the formation of the sun, accretion was taking place, which involved molecules and particles colliding and sticking together, building the various planets in our Solar System as we know it today.

It is estimated that over one-hundred-trillion large asteroids and planetesimals existed when our planet was formed in the Solar System, colliding together and causing them to combine. As their mass increased; the pull of gravity formed larger planets from debris and particles.

The age of Earth is only one- third the age of the Universe. The events that created the Earth would not have occurred without the sun's gravity. After the formation of Earth, the surface was extremely hot and molten due to volcanism and earthquakes that finally formed the shape and the mass that holds everything together through gravity. The Earth continued to change over hundreds of millions of years, due to asteroid bombardments.

2. The Early Earth.

The early Earth, also known as the first billion years on the geographic time scale, or the Pre-Biotic Earth. The surface of the Earth continued to change during this time. A scientific theory is that the Earth had a twin planet known as Thea on the same orbit, which collided with the Earth.

The collision made the Earth larger, increasing its mass and gravity, and tilting the whole planet to an angle of 23.5 degrees. This allows our seasonal change and may have increased Earth rotation. The collision debris also created our moon. The Earth no doubt had an atmosphere of some kind by now. However, Earth did not yet have a magnetic field, so the solar wind from the sun blew the atmosphere away.

The moon' s formation instigated tidal changes, is essential for the evolution of life and the stability of our planet. Radioactive decay caused heat and gasses to build up in the Earth's core causing volcanoes to form. Releasing various gasses such as carbon dioxide, ammonia and ejecting lava and molten rock. As lava spewed over Earth's surface, evidence of asteroid craters were erased from the surface. Water gas, or vapour ejected from the core through the volcanic activity, also through heavy asteroid collisions with the surface. Vapour rose into the atmosphere combining with other gases in the atmosphere, forming incredibly dense clouds above the Earth. This created a reflective shield, preventing solar heat from penetrating to the Earth's surface.

The oldest rocks provide information of Earth's surface dating back 4 billion years. Metamorphic rocks Called Acasta Gneiss, (rocks that have been modified by extreme heat and pressure), were found in Northern Canada they are composed in part of quartz and feldspar. These minerals are probably derived from metamorphosed granite, itself formed when igneous rocks such as basalt are melted in the presence of water. The composition of the Acasta Gneiss suggests that granitic continents and surface water existed four billion years ago during the formation of Earth.

3, Earth's Core

The planet was hot enough to melt heavy metals with higher densities, which sank to the Earths centre of mass.

The iron catastrophe resulted in the separation of the primitive mantle and a metallic core only ten million years after the Earth began to form, which resulted in the layered structure of Earth and eventually, set up Earth's magnetic field. It is this that continues to protect Earth's atmosphere from solar winds. Earths earlier atmosphere consisted of hydrogen and helium, about 4.4 billion years ago.

4, Water On Earth

Once the asteroid bombardment ceased, the surface of the Earth began to cool. Within one hundred and fifty million years, the dense, immense clouds began to pour rain over the entire planet, cooling the molten rock and creating lakes and oceans. Recent evidence suggests the oceans may have begun to form 4.2 billion years ago. Water erosion began to erase evidence of the enormous craters from the late heavy Asteroid impacts, which covered Earth's surface, and created Earth's solid crust.

5. Tectonic Plates

Plate tectonics are a feature unique to Earth. Scientists argue that tectonic plates may not have existed on Earth before the Archaean Era. Therefore there was some time in the Earth's formation that plate tectonics were conceived and evolved. Some arguments suggest that plate tectonics could not form until the Earth's crust had solidified from its molten state. Seafloor spreading through subduction is the primary driver for plate movement. So the warmer Earth may have had a weaker, less dense lithosphere. The processes of mantle convection may have been different on the earlier Earth.

The Earths lithosphere refers to the crust and the up-permost mantle constituting the hard and rigid outer layer of the Earth.

Zircons as old as 4.4 billion years have been identified and indicate that continental crust was formed very early in Earth's history. This is not necessarily clear evidence that plate tectonics and crustal recycling was taking place. Zircon is a ubiquitous trace mineral, found in sedimentary rocks.

Mantle convection is the process that drives tectonic plates and mid-oceanic ridges through heat flow from the core to Earth's surface. Continental plates were formed.

6, Primordial Atmosphere.

The early Earth Primordial Atmosphere contained almost no oxygen and would have been toxic to humans and most modern forms of life. As mentioned earlier, the carbon dioxide and ammonia, ejected from earlier volcanic activity. Before the Earths, cooling period, increased over billions of years to the level we see in today's atmosphere. After about one billion years from the Earth's origins. Modern life as we know it would not have been possible yet primitive cell life was now possible to form and evolve on Earth. Due to the high temperature of Earth's centre and volcanic activity, the crust emitted halogen gasses, ammonia, hydrogen, carbon dioxide, methane, water vapour, and other gasses in the following one hundred million years. This atmosphere is similar to Titan, one of the larger moons of Saturn today. The primordial atmosphere is believed to have reached a pressure of two hundred to two hundred and fifty atmospheres. What we can call an atmosphere evolved little by little, with a dense gaseous cloud zone.

The process of cooling and consolidation of the Earth's surface was accompanied, by strong volcanic activity. The new atmosphere was formed by strong emissions of methane, hydrogen and nitrogen gasses and water vapour, with smaller amounts of carbon dioxide.

7, The Formation of our Moon

A few scientific hypothesis, exist and are debated on, how the Moon was formed about one hundred million years later than the Solar System and Earth were formed. Some of these hypotheses are:

- Capture hypotheses; suggesting the Moon didn't form near the Earth and was instead, captured in the Earth's gravitation pull maintaining its current orbit.

- 'Co-formation' hypotheses; suggest the Earth and the Moon formed together in the same solar nebula, with the moon remaining the same orbit as today. There are a few problems with that hypothesis, however. If the Moon formed with the Earth, the moon will have the same consistency as the Earth. The Moon is deficient of iron. This hypothesis doesn't explain why the Moon formed one hundred million years after the Earth.

- Giant Impact hypotheses; suggest another, Mars size planet, Thea was on the same orbit as the Earth before colliding. This catastrophic event, sent an enormous amount of debris into Earth's orbit, which coalesced and formed the Moon.

This hypotheses is the most supported as it helps to explain why the Earth has heavier elements than the Moon.

Most astronomers now support the Giant Impact hypothesis as it helps to explain why the Moon is younger than the Earth. It explains the Moon's lower density and lack of Iron and why the Moon is not on the same orbital plane as the Earth. It also explains why the Earth is now on a tilt of 23.5 degrees and why we have seasonal changes.

8, Overview

From the time the Earth first formed, 4.6 billion years ago, the biological and geographical changes, the continuous evolution and the great extinctions, through to the present time is best described as the history of Earth.

Geographical and biological changes have occurred continuously since its formation, and will continue to do so for the next few billion years. Organisms are continuously evolving taking on new forms or becoming extinct in response to an ever-changing Planet.

Plate tectonics have played an important role in shaping the Earth's oceans and continents into the shape we see on today's Earth and all living forms that use them as a habitat. The biosphere in turn, has had a significant effect on the atmosphere and other abiotic conditions on the planet, such as the formation of the ozone layer, the proliferation of oxygen, and the creation of soil. It may be hard to perceive just what the Earth has continued to endure, since its formation through all the eons until today.

Section 3. **First Life**

1. Introduction

Life on Earth is possible, we all know this. We are here and so is every other form of life. Science has identified the basic elements required for life. Science knows that life begins with amino acids.

An experiment in 1952, by Stanley Miller and Harold Urey used water, methane, ammonia and hydrogen. These are the same elements believed to be present in Earths primordial atmosphere when life first occurred.

The chemicals were all sealed inside a collection of sterile glass tubes and flasks connected in a loop. One flask was half full of liquid water and another flask contained a pair of electrodes. The liquid water was heated to induce vapour. Sparks from the electrodes were fired to simulate the lightning through the artificial atmosphere and water vapour. Then the micro atmosphere was cooled allowing the water to condense and trickle back to the first flask in a continuous cycle.

As a result of this experiment, Miller and Urey had observed the mixture had turned pink. At the end of a week, they observed that ten to fifteen percent of the present carbon was now present as organic compounds. Two percent of the carbon had formed amino acids that are used to create proteins in living cells. Nucleic acid was not formed in the reaction. Twenty common amino acids were found to have formed.

In 1961, an experiment performed by Joan Oro, had produced the nucleotide which could be made from hydrogen, cyanide and ammonia, in a water solution. Experiments conducted later showed that RNA and DNA could be obtained through simulated pre-biotic chemistry. Science has proved that life can be created from inorganic matter.

2. Abiogenesis

Abiogenesis. Is the study of how biological life arises from inorganic matter through natural processes. In particular, the term usually refers to the processes by which life on Earth originally arose 3.5 billion years ago. When life first began on Earth it was very primitive.

Amino acids and nucleotides are the building blocks for life. These can form by natural chemical reactions, unrelated to life.

So, life on Earth was possible. Three-point- five billion years ago, the Earth's atmosphere and environment were very different. Modern life would have been impossible. A modern man's chances for survival within a short time would have been extremely bleak.

First oxygen was scarce which would lead to a very short agonizing death, through suffocation. The other chemicals that would have been too acidic for human life and most other forms of life found on Earth today. So. Where did it all come from? Where was the starting point?

3. Building Blocks For Life

At this time in Earth's history, the oceans contained nucleotides and amino acids that existed in little blobs, surrounded by membranes called microspheres. These nucleotides and amino acids we have seen, are essential building blocks for life and DNA or genes.

Although these blobs, were not real cells, they were able to replicate themselves and reproduce chemical reactions from the sun's energy and lightning, producing the nucleotides and amino acids that were then carried to the oceans by rain, thus forming the 'Primordial Soup' containing all ingredients for life. From this Primordial soup arose the microspheres.

4. Symbiogenesis

Symbiogenesis is the study of the merging of two separate organisms, to form a single new organism. Eventually, these microspheres evolved into very simple celled organisms. Bacteria that could feed on chemicals in the water around them. They are called, Heterotrophs, because they could not use sunlight to produce their own food. They gained their energy by converting sugar into substances such as alcohol.

This is the same process used today when making wine in airless environments like wine bottles. The process of fermentation. These cells were prokaryotic because they had no nucleus inside them. Their primitive DNA is contained in the nucleoid.

Today, 3.5 billion years later, bacteria are still prokaryotic.

5. Prokaryotes

Prokaryotes are single-celled organisms, that are able to survive and thrive in various environments, including swamps, wetlands and extreme environments, such as geothermal vents and hot water springs, and (today), in the guts of animals. The typical Prokaryote consists of nine different parts:-

- Capsule - which is found in various bacteria. This is the outer covering, giving the cell protection and assisting it, adhere to other nutrients.

- Cell wall; which helps protect the bacteria and gives it, its shape.

- Cytoplasm; is a gel-like substance containing cell components such as enzymes, salts and various organic molecules. They consist mainly of water. The cytoplasm dissolves cellular waste and helps move material around the cell.

- Plasma Membrane; surrounds the cells' cytoplasm and regulates the flow of substances in and out of the cell.

- Pili: are hair-like structures on the cell that attach to other bacteria cells. Shorter Pili called, Fimbriae help bacteria attach to surfaces.

- Flagella; Long, whip like protrusions that aid in cellular locomotion.

- Ribosomes; cell structures that are responsible for protein production. Ribosomes are organelles, consisting of proteins and RNA. Are also responsible for assembling the proteins in the cell.

- Plasmids: are gene carrying, circular DNA.carrying structures that are not involved in reproduction.

- Nucleiod Region: is the area of the cytoplasm that contains the single bacterial DNA molecule.

Three-point-four billion years ago the oceans were full of prokaryotic bacteria. At this time they still did not use oxygen. There was still very little oxygen in Earth's atmosphere and it remained this way until photosynthesis evolved.

Photosynthesis had a world changing effect on Earth. It is perhaps the greatest step in evolution. It gave bacterial organisms the ability to absorb sunlight and use the energy to make food from the carbon dioxide in the atmosphere. The oceans were very quickly filled with bacteria that could photosynthesize. Making oxygen become more abundant. Early bacterial life introduced oxygen to the atmosphere, as the first free oxygen was released through photosynthesis, by cyanobacteria. It was initially soaked up by iron dissolved in the oceans, forming red coloured iron oxide, which settled to the ocean floor. Over time distinctive sedimentary rocks called banded iron formations were created by these iron oxide deposits. Once the iron in the oceans were used up, about 2.4 billion years ago, the iron oxide stopped being deposited and oxygen was able to start building up in the atmosphere.

6. Stromatolites

The oldest known fossils for any primitive form of life is a bacterial form, known as Stromatolites, dating back over three billion years. Stromatolites can be described in simplistic terms, such as a laminated rock, formed by the growth of blue-green algae or. Cyanobacteria microbes. Stromatolites formed in shallow waters by trapping and binding of sedimentary grains by microfilms of microorganisms.

A Biofilm is composed of a densely packed group of microorganisms. Stromatolites take on various forms or shapes, including conical, stratiform, branching, dome, and columnar types. Some of the oxygen was stimulated by the sun as ultraviolet radiation to form the ozone, which collected in a layer near the upper part of the atmosphere. The ozone layer absorbs a significant amount of the ultraviolet radiation that once passed through the atmosphere. Without the ozone layer ultraviolet radiation bombarding the land and sea, would have caused unsustainable levels of mutations in exposed cells.

Stromatolites are primitive organisms. Lacking a cellular nucleus and thrived in shallow, aquatic environments, and built reefs in much the same way as coral does now. The fossil record for Stromatolite spans an extremely long time in Earths history, about Four billion years with the organism possibly occupying every environment on Earth and playing a major role in the evolution of the Earths environment.

An oxygen rich atmosphere, from stromatolites, represents Earth's third atmosphere. There is substantial proof that the rich oxygen atmosphere mixed with the iron-oxide layers in the geological strata, would have turned the oceans green. Oxygen was toxic. Much life on Earth died out, as a result of its level's rise in what is known as the Oxygen Catastrophe.

Resistant forms survived and thrived. Some developed the ability to use oxygen, to increase their metabolism and obtain more energy, from the same food. Today, Stromatolites are almost extinct in both marine and non- marine environments. Modern stromatolites were discovered in Shark Bay, Australia in 1956, and throughout Western Australia, in both marine and non-marine environments. Moreover in some other localities such as Yellowstone National Park, the Bahamas and the Indian Ocean, modern Stromatolites are mostly found in conditions with large saline levels that prevent animal grazing. The oldest fossil record of Stromatolite in microbial origin, dating back 2,724 billion years.

Prokaryotes may obtain energy from inorganic compounds, such as hydrogen sulphide. This enables prokaryotes to thrive in harsh environments, as cold as the snow surface of Antarctica and as hot as undersea hydrothermal vents and land-based hot springs.

CHAPTER THREE

Proterozoic Eon

Section 1. **Proterozoic Eon**

The Proterozoic Eon is a geological Eon, representing a period before the first abundant, complex life on Earth. The name Proterozoic comes from the Greek, and means Earlier Life.

The Proterozoic eon extended from 2.5 billion years ago to 542 million years ago, and is the most recent part of the old informally named Precambrian time.

The Proterozoic consists of three geologic eras. From oldest to youngest:

Paleoproterozoic.- 2,500 to 1,600 million years ago; the time when the continents first stabilised. The time Cyanobacteria first evolved. Cyanobacteria uses the process of photosynthesis to produce energy and oxygen.

Mesoproterozoic. 1600 to 1000 million years ago. The major event is the formation of the continental landmass, Rodinia. The further development of continental plates and plate tectonics. The era saw the development of sexual reproduction, which greatly increased the complexity of life to come. It was also the start of development of communal living among organisms.

Neoproterozoic 1,000 to 542.0 million years ago. Several glaciations, including the hypothesized snowball Earth during the Cryogenian period.

The Ediacaran period, 635 million to 542 million years ago, which is characterized by the evolution of abundant soft-bodied multicellular organisms.

2, Overview

During the Proterozoic, larger continental landmasses continued to form, by the accretion of smaller ones, often leading to extensive mountain building. As the continents began to erode, sediments were washed into the oceans, producing shallow marine environments, where life could flourish and diversify. Many of these life forms developed the ability to photosynthesize. As a byproduct of photosynthesis, they created oxygen. Over billions of years, this oxygen transformed the Earth's atmosphere.

Because oxygen was toxic to some early life forms, many became extinct. Others thrived and evolved into the first multi-cellular organisms, which are preserved as the Ediacaran fauna. Both the beginning and end of the Proterozoic were marked by widespread glaciation.

3. Life

The first advanced single celled, eukaryotes and multi cellular life. macroscopic fossils roughly coincides with the start of the accumulation of free oxygen. This may have been due to an increase in the oxidized nitrates that eukaryotes use.

The blossoming of eukaryotes such as acritarchs, did not preclude the expansion of cyanobacteria. Stromatolites reached their greatest abundance and diversity during the Proterozoic, peaking roughly 1.2 billion years ago.

Acritarchs are small organic fossils dating back 3,200 million years. They display ecological events, such as the predation and the Cambrian explosion.

During the beginning of the proterozoic the atmosphere had 100-1000 times the carbon dioxide content of today's atmosphere, making it more similar to the atmosphere of Mars than the present day Earth.. Relatively abruptly about 2,000 million years ago, oxygen producing photosynthesising single celled organisms evolved, releasing tremendous amounts of oxygen in an event known as, The oxygen catastrophe.

This rusted all exposed iron on the surface, leaving behind geological evidence called, banded iron formations.

It probably also caused mass extinction among organisms unable to deal with such high oxygen concentrations. Towards the end of the Proterozoic, about 8 million years ago, the planet was hit with an ice age, so hard that many paleontologists believe most of the Earth was covered in glaciers. This period is called the Cryogenian, for its low temperatures. Remarkably, life survived, perhaps in slightly warmer lakes, deep beneath the frigid surface, like today's Lake Vostok in Antarctica.

By the end of the Proterozoic, the unicellular ancestors of today's animals, plants and fungi had appeared as well as some primitive blob and stalk like organisms. In general. data about Proterozoic organisms are very scarce in comparison to eras that succeeded it. Lacking hard shells, these organisms did not preserve very well. The most common remnants are mysterious microfossils called acritarchs, which come in a variety of shapes and sizes. They are thought to be the fossils of unicellular photosynthetic protists.

4. Continents

Throughout the history of the Earth, supercontinents have formed, drifted apart, then formed again into supercontinents through plate tectonics. Around 1.1 billion years ago the supercontinent known as Rodinia was forming due to plate tectonics. Rodinia was not the first supercontinent. It was formed by accretion and fragments produced by the breakups of the older super-continent called, Nuna or Columbia, which was formed 2 billion years ago.

After the breakup of Rodinia, about 800 million years ago, it is possible the continents joined again around 550 million years ago. The hypothetical supercontinent is sometimes referred to as Pannotia or Vendia. The evidence for it is a phase of continental collision, known as the Pan African Orogeny, which joined the continental masses of current day Africa, South America, Antarctica and Australia. It is extremely likely, however, that the aggregation of continental masses was not completed, since a continent called Laurentia, which is roughly equivalent to current day North America. had already started breaking off, around 610 million years ago. It is at least certain that by the end of the Proterozoic Eon, most of the continental mass lay united in a position around the South Pole.

Section 2. **Paleoproterozoic Era**

1. Paleoproterozoic Era

This is the earliest and longest part of the Proterozoic, from about 2.5 billion to 1.6 billion years ago. This is the time when Earth's crust finally stabilised. Volcanism in the Archaean had produced mainly basaltic magmas. Volcanoes in the Paleoproterozoic started producing much lighter, siliceous magmas. A lighter rock, which tended to remain on the surface and led to the build-up of large continental land masses by accretion. Almost all life that existed was anaerobic, before the significant increase in atmospheric oxygen. Anaerobic bacteria do not live or grow in the presence of oxygen. Life depended on a form of cellular respiration for metabolism, because it did not require oxygen. At this time, most life on Earth vanished, because atmospheric oxygen in large amounts is toxic to anaerobic bacteria.

The only life that survived was resistant to oxygen, or spent its life cycle in an oxygen free environment. The massive build-up of free atmospheric oxygen is referred to as the Oxygen Catastrophe. The first Eukaryotes appeared at this time.

Paleontological evidence suggests that, 1.8 billion years ago, there were about 450 days in a year, implying that a day consisted of 20 hours as opposed to our 24 hours. Going further back in time you find the Earth's day consisting of 17 hours, with 514 days to the year. The Earth's rotation was at a faster rate.

2. Climate

There were some differences as the Earth was only half the age it is today. Heat in the Earth's interior was greater than today, due mainly to the radiation from the Earth's interior. Also due to the methane and carbon dioxide based greenhouse atmosphere, during the previous Archaean eon.

The oceans were 55 - 85 degrees Celsius. This was partly due to a lower radiation from the Sun.

During the Paleoproterozoic eon, climate changes were as severe as any in Earth's history, From a global high temperature at the beginning, there were three ice ages, producing deep ice in the tropical areas.

Earth's surface environment changed profoundly and irreversibly, with a drop in methane in the atmosphere as compared to the Achaean atmosphere. Not only the oxygenation history, also the occurrence of Palaeoproterozoic, Ice Ages. Oxygen producing cyanobacteria caused a build-up of oxygen.

Oxygen was probably only, 1 – 2 percent of its level today. Banded iron formations were formed by the oxygen forming compounds with iron in rocks, indicating an increase in atmospheric oxygen. They are not found in rocks younger than two billion years old.

There were three ice ages during the Paleoproterozoic, probably caused from the reduced greenhouse gases in the atmosphere and the build- up of free oxygen. Geologists have found no sign of asteroid impact or volcanic eruptions. They have, however, found unmistakable evidence of the first major ice age of the planet, plunging Earth's temperatures to minus 50 degrees Celsius. The environment shift, threatened to extinguish all life on Earth.

3. Life

Between 2.5 billion and 1.6 billion years ago, life on Earth was still in its infancy. Complex organisms such as plants and animals had not yet appeared. The planet however was teeming with microscopic cyanobacteria, which thrived in the temperate and nutrient rich environment.

The evolution of Eukaryotes, was a massive advancement in the evolution of life on Earth. since they include all complex cells and almost all multi cellular organisms. Some scientists suggest they developed approximately, 1.6 billion years to 2.1 billion years ago. Some acritarchs or small organic fossils are known from at least 16.5 million years ago.

Stromatolites formed massive colonies and flourished on the coastline, which formed outcrops in shallow water, depleting the carbon dioxide in the surrounding water through photosynthesis, producing oxygen. Layers of calcium carbonate, continued to be added seasonally to Stromatolites. Very much like tree rings, as the colonies of Stromatolites continued to grow.

Section 3. **Mesoproterozoic Era and Neoproterozoic Era**

1. Mesoproterozoic Era

This is the era marking the middle of the Proterozoic eon. Lasting, from 1,600 to 1,000 million years ago. The first period of Earth's history, with a respectable geological record; the first identifiable continent that was, Rodinia, had formed by the Mesoproterozoic. Significant oxygen levels were rising throughout this era. By then, the oxygen level was about 2 - 4 percent of today's level. The composition of the sea is little understood.

The formation of the supercontinent, Rodinia, produced some significant changes in the Earth. It was the largest landmass to have existed until that time and significantly changed ocean currents which may have led to snowball Earth, later in the Cryogenian period.

The Era is marked also by the plate tectonics and continental plates. By the end of this era, the continental plates that existed are very similar to what exists today. Extensive evidence survives today of massive mountain building. This is the high point or peak of Stromatolites before their decline during the Neoproterozoic Era.

2. Mesoproterozoic Life

The Mesoproterozoic era is the period in the history of life on Earth where sexual reproduction had evolved. During previous eon, cells were replicating themselves. Sexual reproduction is a major component of multi cellular colonies as they are able to better reproduce and more easily build a stable community.

The supercontinent of Rodinia must have been a desolate, stark place as life had not yet progressed from the sea and colonised land. Life was near the land, however, as the oxygen building cyanobacteria, Stromatolites.

With no plant life on land, the centre of Rodinia would have been a flood-plain, with little to obstruct flooding. Silt and sedimentary layers would have accumulated over the years. Today a giant basin of sedimentary rocks known as the Belt Super-group. extends across Alberta, British Columbia. Montana, Idaho and Washington. The belts are mostly sandstone, siltstone, and limestone. They display wonderfully preserved features like cracks, ripples, and fossilised stromatolites.

3. Neoproterozoic Era

This is the last era of the Proterozoic eon, lasting between 1,000 million years to 542 million years ago. The supercontinent of Rodinia was beginning to drift apart, forming oceanic currents. Several glaciations, including the hypothesized Snowball Earth, during the Cryogenian period; the Ediacaran Period, 630 million to 542 million years ago, which is characterised by the evolution of abundant soft-bodied multicellular organisms.

The end of the Neoproterozoic era marks the beginning of the Cambrian period, which is the period that took a great leap in the evolutionary advances on Earth after the Cryogenian Snowball Earth.

4. Neoproterozoic Life

Betweem the 1940s and 1950s paleontologists began finding fossils of multicellular animals that predated the Cambrian boundary. A few of the early animals appear possibly to be ancestors of modern animals. The first appearance of hard-shelled animals, called Trilobites and Archeocyathids. Most fall into groups of frond like animals and stalked animals.

Towards the end of the Neoproterozoic, hard-shelled fauna known as, Small Shelly Fauna, appeared.

Section 4. **Eukaryotes**

1. Endosymbiosis

When two different species benefit from living and working together. When one organism lives inside the other, it's called Endosymbiosis. The Endosymbiotic theory describes how a large host cell and ingested bacteria could easily become dependent on one another for survival, resulting in a permanent relationship over millions of years of evolution.

Mitochondria and chloroplasts, have become more specialized and today they cannot live outside the cell which is certainly worth noting here. In everyday speech, people use the word Theory to mean an opinion or speculation not necessarily based on facts. In the field of science, a theory is a well, established explanation, based on extensive experimentation and observation. Scientific theories are developed and verified by the scientific community and are generally accepted as fact.

Three billion years ago, enough oxygen had built up in the atmosphere for organisms to evolve, which could not only tolerate oxygen, but can use it as a resource to convert food into energy. This process is respiration. Respiration is far more effective than fermentation and as a result the oceans quickly filled with organisms that could use oxygen to convert food to energy.

2. Eukaryotes

A Eukaryote is an organism whose cells contain complex structures, encased in membranes and are formally referred to as Taxon. The defining structure that sets apart eukaryotic cells from prokaryotic cells is the nucleus, in which the genetic material is carried.

Eukaryote cells also carry other membrane bound organelles such as Mitochondria, Chloroplasts and the Golgi apparatus. Organelles have membrane bound internal structures. All forms of complex life on Earth are Eukaryotes, including animals, plants and fungi. Although most species of eukaryote are protist microorganisms.

You may not be immediately familiar with the word, Eukaryote. You most certainly will be aware of what they are. Almost all various life forms you see, including yourself, are eukaryotes. Eukaryotes are microscopic with the appearance of electromagnetic microscopes and molecular biology.

Animals and land plants are large macroscopic, organisms, containing trillions of individual cells. Realising that all organisms are related, Monophyletic defines a recent common ancestor. Eukaryotes appear to be monophyletic. They make up one of three domains of life.

The two other domains of life are bacteria and archaea, which are prokaryotes and have different features from eukaryotes. Eukaryotes represent few of all living things.

In a human body there are ten times more microbes than human cells. Eukaryotes cells are larger than those of prokaryotes having a variety of internal membranes and structures, called organelles, with a Cytoskeleton made out of protein, composed of microtubules, micro-filaments and intermediate filaments all helping to define the cell's organisation and shape. Their DNA or genes are divided into several linear bundles called chromosomes, which are separated by a tubular spindle with nuclear division.

3. Mitochondria

Mitochondria are organelles and contain their own DNA. In general Mitochondria is the energy-generating powerhouse of eukaryotes, where metabolism takes place. Also with several other jobs such as oxidation of fatty acids, amino acid metabolism and the assembly of iron-sulphur clusters. They are cemented or bound by two membranes, the innermost being unfolded to form singular that takes characteristic shapes such as paddle, flat or tube shapes.

Mitochondria, is an ancestral characteristic of eukaryotes. Modern Mitochondria contains every bacterial cell known. During reproduction, the mitochondria is passed down through to the offspring by the mother.

The origin of the Eukaryotic cell is considered a milestone for the evolution of life since they made possible complex cells and multi cellular organisms. After this point many new groups were created, including the divergence of invertebrates and vertebrates, 670 million years ago. From these many groups, it is said that they have evolved to present day organisms.

Section 5. **Snowball Earth**

1. Makganyene Snowball Earth

Just as complex life was evolving on Earth 2.3 billion years ago, the increased oxygen concentrations on Earth caused a decrease of methane or CH4 in the atmosphere. When free oxygen became available in the atmosphere, the concentration of methane could have decreased dramatically; enough to counter the increasing heat from the sun, due to the increased oxygen levels. A counterbalance. 2,220 million years ago, these conditions accumulated to cause a total, Snowball Earth, called the Makganyene Snowball Earth.

2. Conditions

Nearly half way through the Earth's history, the Makganyene snowball ice age. Snowball Earth is a description of the coldest global climate conditions that can be imagined. The entire planet covered with ice from Pole to Pole. Most of the sun's radiation is reflected back into space from the icy surface. The average global temperature would have been minus 50 degrees Celsius. The average equatorial temperature would have been minus 20 degrees Celsius. The equatorial temperature would have been roughly the modern day Antarctic temperature.

Without the moderation effect on the oceans, temperature fluctuations associated with the day, night and seasonal cycles would be greatly enhanced. This low temperature was maintained by the reflective ice, its high albedo resulting in most incoming solar energy being reflected into space. A lack of heat-retaining clouds, caused by water vapour freezing out of the atmosphere, amplified this effect.

3. Thaw

Since the Earth was almost completely covered with ice, carbon dioxide could not be withdrawn from the atmosphere by release of alkaline metal ions weathering out of siliceous rocks.

Over 4 - 30 million years, enough carbon dioxide and methane, mainly emitted by volcanoes would accumulate to finally cause enough greenhouse effect to make surface ice melt in the tropics. Until a band of permanently ice free land and water developed this would be darker than the ice, and thus, absorb more energy from the sun, initiating a, chain reaction.

4. After Effects

Such an extreme environment as the Makganyene ice age, should have killed off any living organism or cells, but it didn't. Instead, it kick-started evolution. With Earth's atmosphere and environment now stabilised, evolution could be described as, evolution on steroids. Before the end of the Proterozoic eon, the Earth would experience two additional Snowball Ice events.

Section 6. **Late Proterozoic**

1. Life On Land

On land, plant, fungal and animal lines had all split. Though as solitary cells, some living in colonies., around one billion years ago, the first multicellular plants emerged, initially they may have resembled sponges, which have totipotent cells, which is the ability of a single cell to divide and produce all the differentiated cells in an organism, or to allow cells to reassemble and replicate themselves and rely on each other. Isolated cells would die. Although little is known about Archaean bacteria, Archaeans, bacteria and Eukaryotes continued to diversify and become more complex organisms and better adapted to their environments. Each domain repeatedly split into multiple lineages.

2. Multi Celled Organisms

Multi cellular organisms have many extra benefits from single celled organisms. They benefit from advantages of scale rather than the properties of single cells. Larger cells can be more mobile. They can pool sensory information, vibration, light and their chemical environment over a wider area. They have a range of competitiveness strategies available for foraging, hunting and more importantly defence. Being multi cellular, makes it possible to develop different abilities and allows the specialisation of issues and organs and opens up many ways of new life, Kidneys, legs, wings, leaves, brains, all of these features and functions need differentiation of cells. A single cell is not able to do it all. Multicellular and differentiation means, some cells can change their function.without disrupting other cells.

The transition from single cell to multi cell was a huge step in the evolution of life on Earth.

3.   The End Of The Proterozoic Era

The end of the Proterozoic, about 540 million years ago, is roughly the time when the first segmented worms and arthropods: insects like beetles, appeared on Earth. Evolution is definitely on steroids, by the end of the Proterozoic Eon it may look as if evolution finally has a foothold on Earth, enjoying the conditions after the first, Snowball Earth. Not quite. Another snowball Earth is imminent.

Section 7. **Cryogenian Period**

1.   Cause

Scientists don't know exactly what caused this glaciation, or what ended it. Its age of 716.5 million years closely matches the age of a large igneous province made up of rocks formed by magma that has cooled, stretching more than 1,500 kilometres from Alaska to Ellesmere Island in far Northeastern Canada. This co-incidence could mean the glaciation was either precipitated or concluded by volcanic activity, as at this time, the supercontinent of Rodinia was breaking apart. The supercontinent Pannotia began to form, because Rodinia was situated on the equator. Rates of chemical weathering increased and carbon dioxide was taken from the atmosphere. is an important greenhouse gas. Climates cooled globally.

2. Effects

The Neoproterozoic, was a time of remarkable diversification of multicellular organisms, including animals. Organism size and complexity increased considerably after the end of the snowball glaciations. This development of multicellular organisms may have been the result of increased evolutionary pressures, resulting from multiple ice-house, hothouse cycles. In this sense, Snowball Earth episodes may have pumped evolution. Alternatively, fluctuating nutrient levels and rising oxygen, may have played a part.

3, Climate

The name of the Geologic period refers to the very cold global climate of the Cryogenian, the Earth suffered the most severe ice ages in its history, during this period.

The Glaciations are called the Sturtian and Marinoan Glaciations. The Sturtian Glaciation persisted from 750 million years, to 700 million years ago. The Marinoan Glaciation, ended approximately 637 million years ago. During these glaciation periods, the oldest known fossils of sponges and therefore animals make an appearance.

Section 8. **Super Continents**

1. Life after the Cryogenian Period

What happened to life forms during the Cryogenian Glacial Period? Life forms called Ediacara biota, were larger and more diverse than ever. Most scientists believe they may have been the pre curser, to the new life forms of the following Cambrian Period.

The taxonomy of most Ediacaran life forms are unclear. Some are proposed as having been ancestors of modern groups of life. Important developments during this period were the origin of muscular and neuron cells. None of the Ediacaran fossils had any sort of hard body like skeletons. These first appear after the boundary between the Proterozoic and Phanerozoic eons.

The Ediacaran Period gets its name from the Ediacaran Hills in South Australia where Geologist Reg Sprigg first discovered fossils of Eponymous Biota in 1946. The type section is located in the Bed of the Enorama Creek within Brachina Gorge, in the Flinders Ranges of South Australia.

2. Pangaea

During this period, continents drifted away, eventually forming a single massive continent, known as Pangaea.. Before splitting again into the current continental landmasses, about 200 million years ago, before the component continents were separated into their current configuration. Its name is derived from a Greek word meaning, entire.

The formation of Pangaea along with other supercontinents, seems to be cyclical through Earth's 4.6 billion year history, unfolding over a period, three times as long as it takes our Solar System to orbit the centre of the Galaxy. Every 500 - 700 million years they clump together. There may have been several others before Pangaea. The fourth-last supercontinent, called Columbia or Nuna. had all previously formed then broken away to form another supercontinent.

This is one of nature's grandest patterns. So what drives this cycle? And, what will life be like next time the continents meet?

3. Continents

The continents move due to circulation in the Earth's mantle, beneath the seven major tectonic plates. Where the plates meet, one is forced below the other, in a process called subduction. This pulls apart the crust at the other side of the plate, allowing new molten rock to well up to the surface to fill the gap. This process means that oceanic crust is constantly being created and destroyed. Because the continents are made from less dense rock than the heavier and thinner oceanic crust that forms the ocean floor they ride higher in the mantle and escape subduction. As a result, the continents hold their shape for hundreds of millions of years, as they glide slowly around the planet. Inevitably though, continents collide and sometimes clump together to form a supercontinent.

Columbia or Nuna broke up and the next supercontinent. Rodinia formed, from the accretion and assembly of its fragments. Rodinia lasted from about 1.1 billion until about 750 million years ago. Its exact configuration and Geodynamic history are not nearly as well understood as the later supercontinents of Pannotia and Pangaea.

At the time Rodinia broke up, it split into three pieces: the supercontinent of Laurasia, the supercontinent of Gondwana, and the smaller congo. Laurasia and Gondwanaland were separated by the Tethys Ocean. Next Laurasia itself split apart to form the continents of Laurentia, Siberia and Baltica. Baltica moved to the East of Laurentia, and Siberia moved Northeast of Laurentia. The splitting also created two new oceans, The Lapetus Ocean and Paleoasian Ocean.

4. Continents of Today

Right now, we are halfway through a cycle. The Pacific is gradually closing, as oceanic crust sinks into subduction zones in the North Pacific. While the Mid-Atlantic Ridge is feeding out new ocean floor as the Americas move apart from Europe and Africa.

Africa is moving Northward heading for the Southern coast of Europe, While Australia is also on its way North towards Southeast Asia. The continents are moving at about Fifteen millimetres per year. Similar to the speed, your fingernails grow.

5. Evidence

The fossil evidence for Pangaea includes the presence of similar and identical species on continents that are now great distances apart. For example, fossils of the therapsid Lystrosaurus have been found in South Africa, India and Australia, alongside members of the Glossopteris flora whose distribution would have ranged from the Polar Circle to the equator, if the continents had been in their present position.

Similarly, the freshwater reptile Mesosaurus, has only been found in localised regions of the coasts of Brazil and West Africa.

The polar ice cap of the carboniferous period covered the southern end of Pangaea. Glacial deposits, specifically till, of the same age and structure are found on many separate continents, which would have been together in the continent of Pangaea.

6. Life On Pangaea

Life in Pangaea will have been extremely harsh. Temperatures would have ranged from 45 degrees to 50 degrees Celsius or 113 to 122 degrees Fahrenheit in the centre of Pangaea, Higher in summer than in winter. Plant life had evolved and extensively colonised the landmass.

Plants actually changed the chemical makeup of the Earth's atmosphere, by giving off oxygen and absorbing carbon dioxide. They also contributed to erosion and the creation of soil. Also, since plants are stationary, they determine where plant-eating animals live.

CHAPTER FOUR

The Phan-erozoic Eon

The Phanerozoic is the most recent eon in Geological terms and continues till today.

Section 1. **Phanerozoic Eon**

1.   The Phanerozoic eon

The Phanerozoic is the major Eon of life on Earth. The Phanerozoic eon consists of three eras: The Paleozoic era, Mesozoic era and Cenozoic era The Phanerozoic is the time when multicellular life greatly diversified into all of its modern forms. This new Eon covers roughly 542 million years to 450 million years ago.

This was the time that abundant animal life has existed and a time when hard shelled animals first appeared on the geologic timescale. It's name comes from the Greek meaning, visible life. It is the time in the history of life on Earth that visible life forms and abundant animal life forms were apparent.

2.Overview

The Phanerozoic is the most recent eon in Geological terms and still continues today.

This was the period when Metazoans started to diversify and multiply greatly. This rapid expansion is sometimes referred to as, The Cambrian explosion. The phanerozoic is a brief period in Earth's history - about half a billion years, a little less than 12 percent of the time of Earth existence, but almost all Metazoan life is confined to this period.

The Paleozoic was a time of dramatic geological, climatic and evolutionary change.

The most rapid and widespread diversification of life in Earth's history was during the Cambrian era. Life started in the ocean but eventually transitioned on to land. By the late Paleozoic, the land was dominated by various forms of organism and great forests of primitive plants covering the continents.

The Mesozoic was a time of tectonic, climatic and evolutionary activity. The era witnessed the gradual rifting of the supercontinent Pangaea into separate landmasses, which would eventually become the seven continents we know and are familiar with today.

The climate of the Mesozoic was varied. Alternating between warming and cooling periods, though generally hotter than it is today. Dinosaurs would become the dominant vertebrate group late in the Triassic period, and would occupy this position for over 150 million years, until their demise at the end of the Cretaceous.

Mammals also evolved during this era, but would remain small and modest until their ultimate rivals, the dinosaurs, disappeared.

The Cenozoic is the era that began in the wake of the Cretaceous, tertiary extinction event at the end of the Cretaceous. It saw the demise of the last non-avian dinosaurs as well as other unique and marine flora and fauna and the end of the Mesozoic era.

The Cenozoic era is ongoing.

2. Life

The discovery of abundant Metazoan fossils in the nineteenth century was the deciding factor for the boundary of the Proterozoic and the Phanerozoic eons.

Metazoan are a major group of multi-cellular animals. Their body structure becomes fixed as they grow and mature. Although some can metamorphose later in life, changing their body structure in much the same way some insects, mollusks and amphibian animals and insects can do today. For example some insects such as the butterfly start as Caterpillars change or metamorphose into a larvae, then emerge as a butterfly.

The Phanerozoic eon spans the time when there is a rapid emergence of a number of animal phyla, the evolution of these phyla into diverse forms unique plants, the development of complex plants and the evolution of fish, the emergence of animals and the development of modern faunas.

Section 2. **Paleozoic Era**

1. Paleozoic Era

This era began 570 million years ago and ended 248 million years ago. Paleozoic, meaning, ancient l, was a time of dramatic change in evolution, climatic and geological conditions.

The Cambrian period, known as, the Cambrian Explosion, saw the most rapid and widespread diversification of life in Earth's history, in which most modern Phyla first appeared.

Fish, anthropods, amphibians and reptiles, all evolved during the Paleozoic. Life transitioned from the sea onto the land.

Towards the end of the Paleozoic, the land was dominated by great forests of primitive plants and a large diversity of organisms, which began to form the ancient coal beds of the major continents. By the end of the Paleozoic, large reptiles and the first modern plants such as conifers had appeared.

2, Evolution of the Eye

One of the major changes in evolution during the Cambrian explosion was the eye. British evolutionary biologist, Richard Dawkins, suggests the eye would have first evolved as a mucus, covered photoreceptor already with a primitive optic nerve or, eye spot, that could detect quality of light, ambient light brightness and distinguish between light and dark.

Eyespots are common in all unicellular organisms, which includes the euglena. The euglena's eyespot, called a stigma, is a small patch of red pigment, which shades a collection of light sensitive crystals together with the leading flagellum.

The eyespot allows the organism to move in response to light and can distinguish day from night. The movement is often toward the light to assist in photosynthesis.

Over evolutionary time, the eye would have required more cells to improve primitive sight. The cells would have created a shallow dent, or a shallow cup to develop a slight curve to allow the light shining on one side, to register in the other side of the curve. This simple method would provide the ability to determine the direction from where the light comes, and to detect the shadow of any predator.

Over time, the curvature of the eye would deepen enough so the top of the curvature would have closed sufficiently to form a small opening. This advance would have made it possible to detect shapes and movement, such an eye would have produced an upside down image but it would have been a definite improvement.

The next step in the evolution of the eye would be to develop a jelly type of mucus over the small opening of the eye cavity. This mucus would have hardened over a short time and created the lens which provided a sharper, clearer image.

Once these fundamental mechanisms are in place there is the ability for a rapid evolution on the eye, through natural selection, over generations. The quality of vision and further modifications to the eye would have been relatively rapid, resulting in the complex eye structure of various animals on land and in the oceans.

Considering the relative short life cycles of the simpler aquatic organisms, the evolutionary progress of the eyes would have progressed through 400,000 generations, meaning the eye would have evolved through less than half a million years. In evolutionary time scale this is a rapid development.

The eye is not perfect by any means. For example, the nerve that carries the visual signal to the brain is in front of the retina, which can obstruct the vision. The human eye also has a blind spot. If a person places a pencil at a five-degree angle to the visual sight, the, the eye cannot detect the tip of the pencil, hence, a blind spot.

An octopus has better vision than humans.

3. Climate

At the beginning of the Paleozoic, the climate was moderate, becoming warmer as the Cambrian progressed., prompting the second greatest sustained sea level rise in the Phanerozoic.

The landmass of Gondwana was moving at considerable speed south so that Africa and South America were directly over the South Pole. The continental shelf marine environment became steadily colder. However, the landmasses that were to become Northern Europe, Russia and Eastern North America and Greenland remained in the tropical zone. while China and Australia lay in waters which were at least temperate. The early Paleozoic ended with a short but severe ice age. This cold spell caused the second greatest mass extinction of Phanerozoic time. Over time, the warmer weather moved into the Paleozoic era.

The middle Paleozoic was a time of considerable stability with the Ice Age. Sea levels had dropped but slowly recovered. New regions of relatively warm, shallow sea floor were created with the merger of Africa and South America with Gondwana. Plants took hold on the continental margins. Levels of oxygen and carbon dioxide dropped, although less dramatically.

The north - south temperature had moderated. The far southern continent of Antarctica and West Gondwana became increasingly less barren. The late Paleozoic era began with a sudden spike in oxygen levels and a dramatic drop in carbon dioxide levels, destabilising the climate and leading to at least one, maybe two Ice Ages. These were far more severe than the earlier brief Paleozoic ice ages, subject to temperature extremes associated with falling sea levels, increased carbon dioxide and general climatic deterioration. It all culminated in the devastation of the Permian extinction.

4. Life

The Paleozoic Era saw a sudden appearance of invertebrate animal phyla in great abundance at the beginning of the Cambrian, a few primitive fish like invertebrates. All the phylum in today's world were represented during the Cambrian period. Some of those representatives included:

Arthropods:-

- Mollusks,

- Lophophorata.

Appeared almost immediately in the Cambrian. Orthoceras, a straight shelled mollusk, the flower like echinoderms and eventually fish, plants and animals moved onto the land, initially only in coastal areas. They did not move further inland until forests grew and established themselves. These lush forests produced oxygen that was 35 percent of the Earth's atmosphere. Today it is 21 percent.

The high oxygen content may have made it easier for the amphibians that also left the water during this time. Some of these Amphibian Tetrapods evolved to two metres in length, before moving further inland. The high oxygen level is also responsible for giant insects, such as the giant dragonfly, centipedes that could grow to 1.8 metres and giant scorpions that grew to over 50 centimetres long.

Near the end of the Paleozoic, an event called the Permian Mass Extinction occurred. At which time about 95 percent of all living things on Earth became extinct!

Section 3. Cambrian Period

1. Cambrian Period

The Cambrian Period is the first geological period during the Paleozoic era. 543 million to 490 million years ago. The Cambrian was named by, Adam Sedgewick in 1835. Cambrian was being the Roman name for Wales where shale and sandstone deposits yield fossils from this time. This deposit zone is known as the Burgess shale. The Cambrian is unique for its high proportion of sites of exceptional preservation; soft-celled organisms are preserved as well as hard-shelled organisms. As a result, the scientific understanding of the Cambrian biology is clearer than any other time in, the history of life on Earth.

The Cambrian period marked a huge step in the evolution of life on Earth. Before the Cambrian, life was small and simple; complex organisms became common during the previous millions of years.

The Cambrian period is commonly referred to as, The Cambrian Explosion, which will forever make the period a special period in the geographic time scale for palaeontologists.

This vast increase in diverse forms of life produced the first representatives of many modern phyla, representing the evolutionary stems of modern groups of species. The land was still barren as life still prospered in the oceans. Soils were forming on land as a microbial sludge known as soil crust covered the land.

It is not well known why the Cambrian period triggered such a massive explosion in evolutionary diversification. It is suggested that the sudden Precambrian boom was triggered by massive increases in deep sea oxygen levels, and plenty of organic matter from the melting glaciers spanning from horizon to horizon. The land resembled deserts; the sea was relatively warm and the Polar ice was absent from much of the Cambrian Period.

2. Climate

As expected, the climate at the beginning of the Cambrian was cold, as it was the end of the Cryogenian snowball effect. Over time however, the temperature gradually warmed globally, making the oceans a good place to live and allowed many species to diversify. The continents were still forming and were mainly barren rocks. The land had no form of plant or animal life on it yet.

The climate is believed to have been ideal for the diversification of life as the levels of oxygen from photosynthesising Cyanobacteria and algae were at levels needed to fuel the growth of more complex body structures and ways of living.

A warming climate made the environment more hospitable. Rising sea levels, were flooding low-lying land areas forming shallow marine habitats ideal for spawning new life forms.

3. Life

The Cambrian saw an explosion of life forms, mostly invertebrates. One species was common and plentiful. The Trilobites which left a huge amount of fossil evidence. An arthropod with a tough outer skin, the Trilobite was also one of the first animal species to have eyesight. There were more than a hundred types of Trilobites during the Cambrian period.

Worms, mollusks, sponges and echinoderms filled the Cambrian seas. Many of the creatures in the seas developed hard structures for defence. The Wiwaxia for example, that had hard shells, scales and spikes covering the outside of the skull. They lived on the sea floor. Animals now swam, crawled, burrowed, hunted, defended themselves and hid away.

The Cambrian had giant shrimp-like Anomalocaris, which were predators that trapped prey with fearsome mouthparts, lined with hooks. The five eyed, Opabinia was stranger still, catching its victims using a flexible clawed arm attached to its head. These predators hunted along the seabed.

Cambrian mud slides beneath the sea, buried and fossilised soft bodied creatures such as marine worms, sponges and crustaceans.

Plant life during the Cambrian period, was mostly simple, single celled Algae. The single cells often grew together to form large colonies. looking more like one large plant.

Another fossil site similar to the Burgess Shale in Wales is in Chengjiang, in China. This site contains similar type of fossil, to those found in the Burgess Shale, the oldest such fossils ever found, containing organisms with soft-bodied parts. Over a hundred specimens have been extracted by palaeontologists of Trilobites, worms, sponges and various ancestors of crustaceans.

At the beginning of the Cambrian, small skeletonised creatures existed, such as sponges and Mollusks, by the end of the period, these life forms had diversified and Trilobites, Brachiopods, Archaeoocyathids and Echinderms had also evolved.

4. Cambrian Mass Extinction

The Cambrian period came to an abrupt end with a mass extinction, which devastated the Trilobites. Two main hypotheses exist as to why the Cambrian ended with a mass extinction.

The Glacial cooling hypothesis and the oxygen depletion hypothesis.

- Glacial cooling hypothesis; developed by James F. Miller of Southwest Missouri State University states evidence has been uncovered in South America, dating back to the Cambrian-Ordovician boundary. The Ordovician being the period after the Cambrian period.

Sedimentary evidence suggests a decline in global climatic conditions resulting in those fauna unable to tolerate cooler conditions to become extinct. Cooler water temperatures caused a mass extinction among mostly warm water species.

Miller suggests that glacial advance would bring freezing water into shallow marine environments, resulting in the withdrawal of shallow seas and reducing the marine habitat for species intolerant of colder, deeper waters.

- Oxygen depletion hypothesis has been advanced by several geologists, primarily Allison Palmer and Michael Taylor of the U.S. Geological Survey and James Stilt of the University of Missouri. Oxygen depletion would occur when cool waters from deep zones of the oceans spread onto the continents. This would result in the elimination of all organisms not able to tolerate cool conditions and also in stratification of the water column. Species would ultimately perish due to their inability to tolerate dramatic shifts in such limiting factors as temperature and oxygen availability.

Section 4. **Ordovician Period**

1. Ordovician Period

This is the second geological period during the Paleozoic era lasting from 488.3 until 443.7 million years ago. The Ordovician Period was named by Charles Lapworth Jr, in 1879, after the Celtic tribe of the Ordovices. Lapworth recognised some of the fossil fauna in the North Wales strata were different from Alan Sedgewick's previous findings.

The name Ordovician officially received international sanction by the International Geological Congress in 1960.

Life continued to evolve and flourish during this period although this period was also marked by significant mass extinction. Invertebrates mainly mollusks and arthropods dominated the oceans. Fish, the first invertebrates, continued to evolve and those with jaws may have first appeared late in the period. Life had not yet diversified onto land.

During the Ordovician mass extinction, 60 percent of marine species became extinct.

2. Climate

During the Ordovician period, the sea levels were high. The southern continents collected into a single continent called Gondwana. Volcanic activity, spewed massive amounts of carbon dioxide into the atmosphere and the Lapetus ocean, forming North America and the Appalachian Mountains.

This extra carbon dioxide, turned Earth into a hothouse. The marine waters are assumed to have been around 45 degrees Celsius, restricting the diversification of complex multicellular organisms. Over time however, the climate became cooler. Around 460 million years ago, the ocean temperatures became comparable to those of present day equatorial waters. The continent Gondwana was relatively mainly covered with shallow seas during the Ordovician which encouraged organisms to grow and to deposit calcium carbonates that formed and hardened their shells.

Land masses we now know as Africa and South America, were at this time situated at the South Pole and covered in ice caps.

3. Life

Life continued to flourish through the Ordovician and the end of the period. plankton forms, such as conodonts and graptolites were serious affected by the mass extinction at the end of the Ordovician Period. Other species such as trilobites and endocerid cephalopods completely died off.

Numbers of asaphida, brachiopods, bryozoans and echinoderms were greatly affected.

The colonisation of land by plant species would have been limited to shoreline areas. Plants probably evolved from green algae similar to sea moss. Fossil spores from land plants have been identified in Ordovician sediments. Shoreline land plants would have been fungi, which played an important role in facilitating the colonisation of land. Fossilised fungi have been found in the Ordovician, dating back about 460 million years.

4. Ordovician Mass Extinction

The mass extinction at the end of the Ordovician period has been recognised as the second most devastating mass extinction of marine communities in the history of Earth, causing global temperatures to plummet to the lowest levels in the last 600 million years.

Not since the Cryogenian Snowball had life on Earth suffered such extreme climatic conditions. More than a hundred marine invertebrate types perished in this mass extinction including brachiopod and bryozoan species and conodonts, trilobites and graptolite species. along with most reef building fauna.

Palaeontologists have theorised this extinction was caused by the single notion of glaciation of the continental area of Gondwana. Fossilised evidence of the glaciation has been found in the Sahara Desert.

Gondwana passing over the North Pole has been suggested by Palaeontologists as the cause of the glaciation. As large volumes of global ocean water became ice though glaciation, the global water levels decreased.

Thus oceanic temperatures overall became remarkably colder than the middle of the Ordovician period.

The greatest extinctions occurred in the tropical areas which lends support to the premise that, if global ocean temperatures decreased, organisms adapted to warmer tropical conditions would have few options for survival They would have decreasing options of environments capable of accommodating their migration.

Fewer extinctions occurred towards the mid continental areas of Gondwana, providing further support to the theory that glaciations were primarily centred, around the polar regions, during the end of the Ordovician period.

Section 5. **Silurian Period**

1. Silurian Period

This period is the third geological period of the Paleozoic era. Lasting from 443.7 until 416 million years ago. It was named Silurian period by Sir Roderick Impey Murchison in the 1830s. He was examining fossil bearing sedimentary rock strata in South Wales. He named the period after a Celtic tribe in South Wales called the Silures.

The Silurian Period is regarded as, a significant evolutionary milestone. witnessing the appearance of jawed and bony fish. Life appeared on land as small, moss-like plants that grew beside lakes, streams, and coastlines.

During the glaciation period marking the end of the Ordovician period the supercontinent of Gondwana had moved further towards the equator, creating relatively stable and warm temperatures and higher sea levels along with large belts of flat land and a few significant mountain ranges that had formed a number of island chains. Thus, a rich diversity of environmental settings was presented.

The supercontinent of Gondwana continued a slow southward drift, during the Silurian. The southern continents remained united during this period.

2. Climate

The Silurian period enjoyed relatively stable and warm temperatures. Sea levels rose continuously throughout the first half of the Silurian period. although they slowly receded during the second half of the period. The highest Silurian sea level was probably around 140 metres higher than the lowest level reached.

The Earth entered an extended hothouse stage and again, warmer waters covered much of the equatorial landmasses. Glaciers had almost vanished having retreated after the Ordovician glaciation. They remained in the area around the poles.

The Earth's climate had stabilised significantly from the previous pattern of erratic climatic fluctuations. Layers of broken shells indicate severe storms, which would have been caused by the warmer oceanic temperatures, just as we are seeing now, with warming ocean temperatures. The climate and carbon cycle appears to be rather unsettled during the Silurian. Which seems to be a pattern, after mass extinctions.

The climate cooled slightly towards the end of the Silurian, but warmed again at the end of the period.

3. Life

Sea life had certainly diversified. Many new species had evolved since the previous glaciation, probably due to the increase of minerals in the oceans after the glacial retreats at the start of the Silurian Period.

The first bony fish had appeared. Fish reached considerable diversity and developed movable jaws. Sea scorpions, some reaching lengths of several metres, prowled the shallow seas. Many of their fossils were found in New York State. Bryozoa, hederelloids, brachiopods, mollusks and trilobites had diversified and were abundant. The first leeches had also appeared during the Silurian period. Land based plant life was finally appearing around watery areas on land such as rivers, lakes and coastlines. As moss, forests, and vascular plants, mainly Cooksonia in the Northern Hemisphere and Baragwanathia in the Southern Hemisphere.

The Silurian is also known as the first period for coral reefs. Over previous eons stromatolites were responsible for any form of reef. During the Silurian, tabulate corals and rugose corals formed these reefs. Tabulate corals lived in colonies that formed tubular- shaped chains. Rugose corals are sometimes referred to as Horn corals, because of their similarity in looks to a bull horn. The huge reefs proved to be a great hiding place and home to the great diversity of fish and completely changing ocean life, creating a completely new ecosystem for marine life.

Section 6. **Devonian Period**

1. Devonian Period

This is the fourth geological period of the Paleozoic era. It spanned a period from 417 to 354 million years ago. The Devonian is named after Devonshire in England where rocks from this period were first studied.

During this period, plant life first started to diversify on land. The first seed spreading plants appeared and quickly formed forested areas on the continents. Forests were able to grow dense and lush, mainly due to vertebrate herbivores. Animal life had not yet transferred to land.

The first ray, finned and lobe-finned bony fish had appeared. About 397 million years ago pectoral and pelvic fins of lobe-finned fish evolved into legs, enabling these fish to start walking on land as tetrapods, the early ancestors of amphibians.

Primitive sharks became more numerous in the oceans. The first ammonite mollusks first appeared. Coral Reefs were still very common. Another mass extinction at the end of the Devonian Period severely affected marine life.

2. Climate

The Devonian Period is referred to as the Age of Fish, also often referred to as, the Greenhouse Age. Earlier Devonian Age discoveries came from the strata of North America and Western Europe, which during the Devonian Period had straddled the equator as part of the continent of Euramerica.

During the early Devonian, the climate was warm and most probably lacked glaciers. Reconstruction of tropical sea surface temperatures suggests an average temperature of 30 degrees Celsius.

Throughout the Devonian period, carbon dioxide levels dropped steeply which may have been due to the new forests drawing carbon dioxide out of the atmosphere into sediments. This may also have resulted in a cooling period by the mid Devonian, until the temperatures reached as low as 5 degrees Celsius. The climate warmed again towards the end of the period until temperatures again reached the same levels as the beginning of the Devonian.

There is no evidence of corresponding carbon dioxide increased concentrations towards the end of the period, although a range of extant evidence such as plant distribution, does point to late Devonian warming. Dominant organisms in reefs could have been affected by the warming trend. In warmer periods, microbes would have been the main reef forming organisms, whilst in colder periods stromatoporoid sponges would have dominated the reefs.

As the continent of Euramerica drew closer to Gondwana the Devonian climate would have been affected and as early stages of supercontinent Pangaea developed, oceanic currents would have changed, affecting climatic conditions.

3, Life

The warm temperatures of the Devonian meant land conditions were extremely good for plants. They developed vascular tissues, which allowed them to draw water from the soil through a root system and leaves. Such advancements as a root system, allowed trees to grow to heights of 9 metres.

The most dramatic advancement was the seed. Now plants were not dependent of water for reproduction and were able to move further inland. Ferns and trees were capable of covering the land, creating inland microsystems as forests.

Devonian tree stumps at the Gilboa National Park, United States

Lignin evolved towards the end of the Devonian facilitating the development of bark on trees for protection against climatic conditions and straight growth. The forested areas made wonderful habitats for the first spiders, wingless insects and tetrapods.

As already stated, the Devonian period is commonly referred to as The Age of Fish. It is especially notable for the thousands of fish species that evolved during this time. Fish fossils found in Devonian rocks indicate, at the beginning of the period that they had no jaws and the support structure was made of cartilage. These animals appear in rocks. During the period, these fish had developed paired fins, jaws and gills. These were the placoderms.

A huge predator of this period is the, Dunkleosteus, which could grow up to 10 metres in length. Instead of teeth, it had large bony plates that stuck down at the front of its mouth opening. These powerful plates were deadly to other fish and sharks. Jawed fish dominated the seas later in the Devonian Period.

The evolution of the shark came about during the Devonian. It was thought they evolved from the earlier placoderms that had been unable to form bone for the skeleton. Placoderms may have needed to evolve because of competition with other fish species for food. There is little fossil evidence for these sharks, however there is evidence of their teeth. Much of the evidence is based on many different types of fossil remains of shark teeth.

Bony fish, the lobe-finned variety appeared in the oceans during the Devonian. They had pairs of fins with fleshy lobes on the base and more typical fin membranes at the ends; the lobes contained jointed bones, thought to have evolved into legs. This development essentially accommodated the transition of these fish into amphibians, able to live successfully on land and in the water. Eventually they diversified to become completely land based, becoming our common ancestors.

Lung-fish were among the numerous fish species of the Devonian Period. In numerous ways the lung-fish looked like the bony fish, including fins, with flesh towards the end of its fins. The major difference being that lung fish, as the name suggests, had developed lung sacks which drew air from the gills, leading from the throat. This species was able to adapt to different climatic conditions on land and in the oceans.

Shallow coastal waters provided the right conditions for the establishment of a vast diversity of reefs on a scale never repeated in the history of life on Earth. Reefs are generally built up by various carbonate, secreting organisms with wave resistant frameworks.

The Devonian reefs are composed from calcareous algae, stromatoporoids, tabulate and rugose corals, all sponge like species. Their work continued throughout the Devonian period. They built some of the largest reef systems in the world.

Invertebrates developed well during the Devonian. The Ammonite is one, of which many various species evolved.

4, Devonian Mass Extinction

Just as life, both in the oceans and land, were diversifying with various species the Devonian Period ended in a mass extinction affecting ocean habitats far more than land based habitats. Sponge varieties and the coral species in particular were affected and as a result of this extinction, massive coral building will never again occur on Earth for thousands of years. This affected the fish species that had evolved and developed, depending upon coral reefs for protection and habitats.

Among the species mostly affected, were the brachiopods, trilobites, ammonites, conodons and acritarchs, as well as the jawless fish, placoderms. Land based species, such including plants and anthropod ancestors were unaffected by the mass extinction. There are two hypotheses for the cause of this mass extinction.

First the, glaciation hypothesis which many paleontologists believe resulted from glaciation on the supercontinent of Gondwana, as evidenced by glacial deposits of this age in northern Brazil. These indicate a possible effect replicating the end of the Ordovician period. Global cooling events and the lowering of sea levels, may have triggered the extinction.

And there is the meteorite impact hypothesis. Currently the evidence for this event is inconclusive. The exact cause for the Devonian Mass Extinction is still being debated.

Section 7. **Carboniferous Period**

1. Carboniferous Period

The Carboniferous is the fifth geological period of the Paleozoic era. Lasting from 359.2 until 299 million years ago, named after the two Latin words. Carbo, meaning, coal and, Ferre meaning, carry. The Period was named by, geologists, William Conybeare and William Phillips in 1822. The name reflects the fact that many coal beds were formed globally during this time, especially northern Europe, Asia, mid-western and eastern North America.

Both plant and animal species were well established on land, amphibians were the most dominant animal species among vertebrates, of which one branch would eventually evolve into reptiles.

The first unique vertebrate was the anthropod, which had become very common and many were much larger than they are today. Large, lush forests now covered the land. As the name of the period, Carboniferous infers, much of this forest would eventually be laid down to become the present day coal fields.

The oceans were by now recovering from the mass extinction that affected marine life at the end of the previous period. In the middle of this period, yet another extinction affected the marine environments, particularly impacting ammonites and crinoids. This minor extinction, was caused by global warming.

Supercontinent Gondwana had completely broken away by now and the smaller landmasses were drifting towards creating the supercontinent of Pangaea.

The Carboniferous period was a time of mountain building when the collision of the Euramerican and Gondwana land-masses uplifted and created the Appalacian mountains, the Hercynian mountains and the Ural Mountains.

The early part of the Carboniferous was mostly warm. In the later part of the period the climate cooled dramatically.

2. Climate

The initial break up of the supercontinent of Gondwana caused instability of the Carboniferous climate. The effects of the late Devonian mass extinction also affected the early climate of the Carboniferous period. The period began, with relatively hot climatic conditions, with an average global temperature of 20 degrees Celsius. Generally, however, there was a trend towards milder global temperatures except for a slight glitch, midway through it when the temperature dropped to 12 degrees Celsius, which was ideal for the formation of coal.

The Carboniferous period and today's Quaternary period are the only periods in Earth's history that have shared the same average global temperatures. Today's average global temperature is 15 degrees Celsius.

The middle of the Carboniferous period suffered an ice age, due to climate change. Great sheets of glacial ice, thousands of feet thick, accumulated - melted - then accumulated again in cycles, as the Earth cooled and rewarmed.

At the South Pole, glaciers up to 2400 metres thick existed. Then gravity, combined with their weight, moved them to lower elevations, destroying and pulverising everything in their path. Ancient bedrock in Africa, Australia, India and South America show scratches and gouges from this glaciation.

3. Life

Land based plants and trees were developing strong root systems. enabling them to grow larger and occupy more land, including drier land.

Trees were growing taller and below their canopy of branches and leaves other environments were evolving. The plant life was literally changing the atmosphere by pumping more oxygen into the air.

Swampy forests were preserved as major coal beds, giving the Carboniferous period the name.. The fronds of some Carboniferous ferns are almost identical with those of today's species, though some Carboniferous ferns, such as, Pecopteris, Cyclopteris, Neuropteris and alethopteris were large tree ferns. Other trees and plants ranged from low growing varieties at thirty centimetres to giants such as the Cordaites thirty metres tall. The Cordaites have strap like leaves and are early relatives of today' conifers.

Giant Millipedes lived on the forest floor and giant insects took to the air.

Amphibious Tetrapods became diverse. Some adapted to spending more time on land, while others returned to the water. From the Tetrapods evolved another group of land vertebrates. The early reptiles.

The glaciations, which plagued the Middle Carboniferous, devastated the swampy rain forests.

The Carboniferous period saw the evolution of the first true bony fishes, the first sharks and the first amphibians. It also was the period during which the first Amniotes appeared. The amniotic egg, the defining characteristic of amniotes, enabled the ancestors of modern reptiles, birds, and mammals to reproduce on land and colonise unique habitats that were previously uninhabited by vertebrates.

The fact that the oxygen concentration in the Earth's atmosphere in the Carboniferous was 30 percent, much higher than today's concentration of 21 percent, enabled land species, such as arthropods, to grow larger and insect forms to diversify and grow to exceptional sizes.

There was the Giant Dragonfly, which grew wingspans of seventy-five centimetres and the gigantic Pulmonscorpius. which was a species of scorpion that grew to

70 centimetres in length. Numerous species of giant insects have been found in the coal fields of Saarbrucken in Germany and from the hollow trunks of fossil trees in Nova Scotia. Some British coalfields have yielded good specimens. Tetrapod fossils are common in coal. These animals came in various forms from small eel-like amphibians that were fully aquatic to giants as large as Crocodiles.

Amphibious Tetrapods became very common during the Carboniferous, more so, than they are today. Some were up to six metres in length. These had long bodies with weak, undeveloped limbs and a head covered with bony plates.

 Some lived in swamps, ponds, lakes and rivers, others were semi aquatic. The decimation of the rain forests during the mid Carboniferous glaciations slowed the evolution of amphibians, as they could not adapt and survive in the cooler, drier conditions. Fungi still existed and continued to diversify in marine environments. All modern species of fungi existed during the Carboniferous.

The amount of space available for marine life declined, due to the large Carboniferous glaciations. because the presence of two large ice sheets at the southern pole which sucked up large amounts of water and locked it away from the oceans as ice lead to the global sea levels fluctuating – in turn directly leading to the extinction of shallow water marine invertebrates.

Low-lying swamps also dried up. Then as the glaciers and ice sheets receded, these shallow water marine environments along with the low-lying swamp environments refilled with water.

The extinction event at the end of the Devonian period saw the demise of giant fish species, such as the Placoderm leaving sharks to become the dominant predator of the Carboniferous oceans. Many sharks had crushing teeth for breaking hard shelled Brachiopods, Crustaceans and other marine organisms. Other sharks had piercing teeth, and some had cutting teeth. Most sharks were marine species. Some lived in coal swamps.

Nautilus developed variations with great numbers in the marine environments. Some bony fish, apart from living in coastal water, diversified into rivers and other fresh water environments.

4.   Mid Carboniferous Extinction

Compared to the previous glaciations during the Paleozoic era the Mid Carboniferous Extinction event was, mild. This glaciation, caused by global climate change, was primarily by the breakup and movement of the supercontinents formerly known as Gondwana and massive ice sheets forming in the southern Polar region.

The major effect this event had on land was the demise of the swampy rain forests which Palaeontologists affectionately refer to as 'The Carboniferous Rainforest Collapse or CRC'. Ultimately, this would form the coal fields of today. As was experienced in the last extinction event during the Devonian period. This extinction affected the shallow marine environments hardest. The sea levels fluctuated repeatedly. The shallow coastal water retreated, exposing the coral reefs and killing the organisms, which created the reefs thus affecting the fish and other organisms that rely on the reefs for protection and habitat.

Section 8. **Permian Period**

1. Permian Period

The Permian is the sixth geological Period, of the Paleozoic era.

Occurring 299 million until 251 million years ago and was the last period of the Paleozoic era.

As with the previous Silurian period, the Permian Period was named by Sir Roderick Impey Murchison who, in 1841 was President of the Geological Society of London. He had identified typical strata in extensive Russian explorations. Murchison named the period after the ancient kingdom of, Permia. The region now lies in the Perm Krai, in Russia.

The Permian period was primarily hot and dry. The Period was dominated by the supercontinent known as, Pangaea.

The rain forests of the previous Carboniferous period had vanished, leaving behind, large areas of desert. The Paleozoic era had ended with a massive Extinction event. The Permian Extinction was the largest mass extinction the Earth has ever seen. It affected many groups of organisms in many different environments, heavily impacting marine communities and causing the

extinction of most marine invertebrates of the time –
this seriously compromised the history of life on Earth.

The event resulted in total extinction of 90 percent of
all marine species and 70 percent of all land species or,
90-95 percent of all life on Earth, though, in diminished
numbers, some species managed to survive the extinction, they never again reached the ecological dominance they had before it. The Permian was a time of
great changes and life on Earth after the Permian was
never the same again.

2. Climate

At the start of the Permian, Earth was still in the grip of
an ice age, from the Carboniferous. The Polar regions
were covered with deep layers of ice. The overall temperature during the Permian period was cooler as the
supercontinent of Pangaea had fully formed and was
moving northward towards the North Pole.

Mountains formed as Pangaea moved. The Ural Mountains were pushed up by the collision of Euramerica
and Siberia in Pangaea's final period of formation.
Much of the land mass was dry. Pangaea was so large
that the interior did not benefit from the ocean waters.
Most of the interior land was desert as Pangaea was so
huge. Temperatures were extreme, ranging from very
hot to very cold in the interior.

A significant factor in the Permian was the dramatic
drop in oxygen levels. After reaching its high, during
the Carboniferous, Oxygen began to disappear from
both the atmosphere and the oceans, severely impacting

all walks of life with one exception: plants, which thrive on carbon dioxide.

The rising carbon dioxide levels most significantly affected the plants. For a while, when the carbon dioxide levels were rising, the plants thrived but as the world became warmer and drier the plants could no longer cope with the excessive heat and aridity.

The sea levels of the Permian Period remained generally low as a result of the Polar regions being covered in thick Ice layers which may have helped, result in the mass extinction of many marine organisms that prefer shallow coastal areas. Three general areas are especially noted for their extensive Permian deposits. The Ural Mountains in Russia, where Perm itself, is located. This is the same area where Sir. Roderick Impey Murchison made the studies mentioned earlier. The Permian Basin, in Texas. Is so named because it has one of the thickest deposits of Permian rocks in the world.

3. Life

The changing climate also affected how animals were evolving. Early reptiles were well placed to adapt to the new environment of the Permian period, shielded by their thicker, moisture retaining skins, they moved where amphibians had previously been dominant after their migration to the land, during the Carboniferous period. Gradually the reptiles became ideally suited to the desert type habitats in which they thrive today.

The cold-blooded reptiles, had to find ways to deal with temperature variations from below freezing at night to over 38 degrees Celsius, during the day. Some of the primitive Pelycosaurs, which grew up to three metres in length had sail like structures on their backs, which are thought to have acted as heat exchangers by catching the sun in the morning to help warm the slow and clumsy creatures.

During the late Permian period more metabolically active reptiles became dominant. These reptiles, known as Therapsids, found an internal solution to keep themselves warm. Scientists believe they eventually became warm blooded. Conserving heat generated through consumption of their food. These more metabolically active reptiles, adapted for the harsh interior regions of Pangaea.

Reptiles grew to dominance among vertebrates. It is believed that it was from these reptiles the first Mammals would appear.

The Permian period experienced lower sea levels. On land, the swamps dried up and many of the plants that needed water died out. New plants developed that adapted to the dryer conditions. One of these was the early ancestor to today's Ginko.

Most of the trees that covered large areas of Pangaea, were conifers. The oceans of the Permian period became dominated by bony fishes, with fan shaped fins and thick heavy scales. There were large reef communities that harboured nautiloids, which resembled squid. Ammonoids, with their tightly coiled, spiral shells are also widespread in the Permian fossil record. Marine deposits representing the Permian period are rich in fossils such as: mollusks, echinoderms and brachiopods.

Trilobites, and a host of other marine groups by the end of the Permian Period, had become extinct.

4. Permian Period Mass Extinction

Palaeontologists record the end of the Permian period as the most extensive extinction event in Earth's history or 'The Great Dying', the period when 90-95 percent of all species, became extinct. The Permian Extinction is also the only mass extinction of insects, and larger than the later Cretaceous Extinction which saw the demise of the Dinosaurs. The actual cause of the extinction at the end of the Permian remains in debate. Numerous theories have been forwarded in explanation.

One theory puts the supercontinent of Pangaea as the cause: • The reduction of continental shelves would have presented competition for space. This is hotly debated, as it presents no answer why the extinction event occurred at the end of the Permian period. Pangaea had existed throughout the era.

5, Glaciation:

A possible mechanism for the extinction is the rapid warming and severe climatic conditions causing fluctuations by concurrent glacial events in the North and South Poles.

6, Volcanic Eruptions:

Palaeontologists believe the Extinction was the result of basalt eruptions in Siberia. These eruptions were large and sent a quantity of sulphates into the atmosphere. These volcanic eruptions may have been rich in silica as evidence in China supports, making these eruptions very explosive and sending large ash clouds around the world. The combination of sulphates in the atmosphere and the ejection of ash clouds may have lowered global climatic conditions. The age of the lava flow in Siberia, and a study of uranium and lead contents in zircons from rock found in south China, supports this theory.

CHAPTER FIVE

Age Of The Dinosaur

Section 1. **Mesozoic Era**

1. The Mesozoic Era

The Mesozoic Era meaning, 'middle life', 250 million years ago, was a time of tectonic, climatic and evolutionary activity. That era saw the gradual drifting of what was the supercontinent Pangaea, into the separate landmasses that we see today.

During the Triassic period, dinosaurs would become the dominant vertebrate, and remain dominant for the next 150 million years, until their demise towards the end of the Cretaceous period. Mammals evolved during this era, but remained small and modest until their rivals, the dinosaurs, vanished.

The climate of the Mesozoic alternated between warming and cooling periods. Overall the temperatures were warmer than they are today.

2. Climate

The climate during the Mesozoic era was so warm that there were no ice caps at the Poles. Plant life flourished extremely well in the warm, moist environment. Temperatures varied as the supercontinent Pangaea was in the process of drifting apart. This was resulting in more landmass becoming accessible to the sea.

Temperatures continued to increase before stabilising, causing humidity levels to rise within the proximity of water; deserts retreated. The climate of the Cretaceous however is less certain and is widely disputed. It is thought that higher levels of carbon dioxide in the atmosphere may have caused a temperature gradient from the north to the south to flatten making a universal temperature across the Earth.

Temperatures, on average, were 10 degrees Celsius higher than today. By the middle of the Cretaceous, equatorial waters may have been as high as 20 degrees Celsius in the deep ocean. The equatorial waters may have been too warm for sea life, making the equatorial land areas deserts despite their proximity to water.

The circulation of oxygen to the deep ocean may also have been disrupted. Large volumes of organic matter accumulated, unable to decompose and eventually being deposited as black shale, a dark coloured mud rock containing organic matter. Black shales have formed throughout Earth's history in all parts of the world. Shale typically exhibits varying degrees of fissility breaking into thin and often splintery layers and usually parallel to the otherwise indistinguishable bedding plane, because of parallel orientation of clay mineral flakes.

3. Life

By the Mesozoic era, life is rapidly diversifying and beginning to look very familiar. The dominant animals on land and oceans are reptiles. The most well known being are the Dinosaur. Dinosaurs began in the Triassic, spreading by the Jurassic, then dominating the Cretaceous.

The Mesozoic is known as 'The Age Of Reptiles' because the dinosaurs are so prominent. Other life forms are present on the planet at this time, birds and mammals also appear during the Mesozoic.

Deciduous trees and flowering plants also appear over the landscape, which was dominated by various plant species such as gymnosperms, which are vascular, cone-bearing non-flowering plants, such as conifers that produce seeds with no coating. These differ from Earth's current flora, in which the dominant land plants with number of species are Angiosperms. One particular plant species, the Ginkgo Biloba, is perceived to have evolved at this time and still exists today as the only surviving species from its phylum. The Sequoia is also believed to have evolved in the Mesozoic.

4. Continents

At the beginning of the Mesozoic, Africa was joined to the supercontinent of Pangaea, sharing the fauna, which was dominated by Theropods, Prosauropods and primitive Ornithischians, by the close of the Triassic period. Late Triassic fossils are found throughout Africa, but are more common in the south as opposed to the north. The boundary separating the Triassic and Jurassic marks the occurrence of an extinction event with global effect., although African strata from this period have not been thoroughly studied.

About half way through the Mesozoic Era, the little island country now known as Madagascar separated from Africa, but stayed connected to India and the rest of Gondwana landmass. During the Cretaceous, India and Madagascar separated from Gondwana landmass, until they reached their present positions.

5. The End Of The Mesozoic Era

The end of the Cretaceous marks the end of the Mesozoic era. The end of the Cretaceous is a time of mass extinction for many animal groups. The dinosaur, marine reptiles such as the Plesiosaurs, Ichthyosaurs and Mosasaurs, along with the flying reptiles including the Pterosaurs; all became extinct by the end of the Cretaceous Period, along with Invertebrates, such as Ammonites and Belemnites.

There is strong evidence that global cooling occurred at the end of the Mesozoic. The cooling may have been caused by a huge asteroid impact near the Yucatan peninsula, and a large number of volcanic eruptions in the area that is today, India and Pakistan. The sun's rays would have been blocked for some time by the debris spewing into the atmosphere.

Section 2. **Triassic Period**

1. Triassic Period

The Triassic Period is the first geological period, of the Mesozoic Era, spanning from 248 million until 206 million years ago.

The Triassic period was named by, geologist. Friedrich Von Alberti in 1834. It comes from the Latin word Trias, from a three layered division of rock types. Red beds capped with chalk, followed by black shale. These are found in Germany and N W.Europe.

The early half of the Triassic witnessed life's slow recovery from the extinction at the end of the Permian Period. The rise of Archosaurs to dominance characterised the second half of the period.

The first true mammals also evolved during the Triassic, as well as the first flying vertebrates, the Pterosaurs.

The gigantic supercontinent Pangaea still existed at the beginning of the Triassic, but in the second half of the period started to drift apart into separate landmasses.

Global temperatures during the Triassic were mostly hot and the atmosphere dry. The Earth became colder and wetter when Pangaea drifted apart.

2. Climate

The Climate of the Triassic was semi-arid, to arid and very seasonal. There were still no polar ice caps yet. The climate was punctuated by violent monsoons.

The supercontinent, Pangaea, fused together, containing all known present day continents. until the gigantic landmass began drifting northward. Pangeas's size, limited the moderating effect of the global ocean.

The Polar regions would have been moist and temperate, due to their lack of ice sheets. The oceans were vast as the only landmass, Pangaea was limited to the bottom of the southern hemisphere and the lower top of the northern Hemisphere.

Pangaea's size and shape prevented moisture from the Panthatassia ocean from reaching the internal regions. As a result these were scorching hot desert areas. Some other regions of the Earth such as New Zealand, which were marine environments before the Triassic period, were beginning to rise from the sea through volcanic activity in the southern hemisphere.

Oxygen levels during the first half of the Triassic were low due to the previous Permian extinction; about 15 percent as compared to 21 percent today. Triassic rocks found in Antarctica. bear a rare green mineral, known as Berthierine which cannot form when oxygen levels are high.

By mid -Triassic, oxygen levels had risen to 18 percent, possibly due to the increasing number of plants pumping oxygen into the atmosphere, through photosynthesis. By the end of the Triassic, however, oxygen levels had again plummeted to levels as low as the Permian period. The lowest levels of oxygen of the late Triassic, were lower than Earth had experienced in previous 500 million years.

Levels of carbon dioxide at the beginning of the Triassic were higher than the previous 350 million years, which indicates a hot climate. These uniformly high levels dropped immensely by mid-Triassic, nearing present day levels and cooling the climate, also resulting in cooler oceanic temperatures. This enabled marine creatures to re-establish in once deserted regions.

3, Life

At the start of the Triassic, newer areas on Earth were rising above the oceans like New Zealand, due to volcanic activity. Fossil records indicate that native flora were colonising the available land. Species such as, Kauri, Totara and Kahikitea trees were dominating the land. due to continued volcanism. Fossil records from strata in Canterbury show that a primitive amphibious lizard known as a Nothosaurus, that could grow to three metres in length, had begun to colonise the land.

Modern forms of coral first appeared during the Triassic period, although not forming the great reefs as in the Devonian period. These reefs were modest by comparison with earlier periods. The great diversity of fish species perished during the Permian extinction and there was uniformity among those in the Triassic.

Not surprisingly the greatest diversity was seen amongst the reptiles as this period is known as 'The Age of Reptiles'. These included Nothosaurus, Sauropterygia and Pachypleurosaurs.

By mid Triassic, Placodonts, the first Plesiosaurs, the lizard-like, Thalattosauria and the very successful, Ichthyosaurs which first appeared in the early Triassic, soon diversified and became very numerous by the end of the period. These reptiles would eventually dominate the oceans and land.

At the beginning of the Triassic, the extremely hot and dry conditions of internal Pangaea, were ideal for reptiles. The cold-blooded reptiles were more successful in hot environments compared to Therapsids, which were the first mammals.

The first dinosaurs evolved from the first reptile-like mammals during the Triassic. True mammals began their evolution during this time. Although they were very small, they did come to dominate after the Cretaceous period. The end of the Triassic saw the first flying reptiles, the Pterosaurs. These flying reptiles were not like modern birds. Dinosaurs of the Jurassic are closer in similarity to modern birds.

Reptiles also dominated the oceans of the Triassic. They had developed lungs for breathing and did not have gills. The Plesiosaurs developed during the Triassic, though not in significant numbers until the Jurassic and Cretaceous periods.

Some of the flora of the earlier Paleozoic era such as the fern like trees, and Lycopods, that dominated earlier landscapes, suffered during the Triassic, unable to survive the climatic conditions.. Others were diversifying and evolving into new species. The Conifers and Ginkgos were further developing over the Triassic.

4, Late Triassic Extinction

The Triassic Period ended with yet another mass extinction, which had greatest effect on the oceans. Conodonts perished along with all other reptiles except the Plesiosaurs and Ichthyosaurs. Invertebrates, such as brachiopods, gastropods and mollusks were severely affected. According to Palaeontologist Jack Sepkoski, 22 percent of marine species, representing about half of the marine life, perished.

For decades it was believed this extinction was caused by volcanic activity, raising land, such as New Zealand, from beneath the oceans, but in recent times the there has been the suggestion that twelve thousand tons of methane rising from under the oceans and releasing into the atmosphere could be the cause. It was reasoned that volcanic activity had been ongoing for 600,000 years, during the Triassic.

The extinction took place over a period of 10,000 – 20,000 years. According to Earth Scientist, Micha Ruhl of the University of Copenhagen, volcanic activity certainly played a minor role as evidenced by carbon found in sedimentary rock, which indicated that this extinction occurred at the same time as a massive methane release into the Earths atmosphere, at the end of the Triassic.

Section 3. **Jurassic Period**

1. Jurassic Period

The Jurassic Period is the second geological period, of the Mesozoic Era. 199.6 million until 145.5 million years ago. The Jurassic period was originally named, Jurakalk in 1795, by Abraham Gottlob Werner. The name, Jura comes from the Celtic root, Jor, which is Latinised into, Juria. - meaning, forest. The term, 'Jurassic' is linked to the, Jura Mountains for its limestone strata, separating the Rhine and Rhone rivers in France, Switzerland and Germany.

At the beginning of the Jurassic period, the Pangaea supercontinent was beginning to separate into various continents, creating ocean currents and exposing more land to the oceans thus causing a change in the Earth's climate, from hot and dry to warm and humid, with many of the hot dry deserts being replaced with lush rain forests.

Dinosaurs began their domination of Earth, peaking during the Jurassic period, as they evolved and diversified into a variety of groups., from the gigantic Sauropods, such as Brachiosaurus and Diplodocus to the medium to large Theropods such as the Allosaurus and Megalosaurus.

The Jurassic also saw the Stegosaurs, such as the Stegosaurus. Early mammals were very small, mouse sized, creatures that were nocturnal. It is possible that the first birds evolved during the late Jurassic. Land dinosaurs were placed in two categories: Herbivores and Carnivores. The most gigantic dinosaurs were the Herbivores.

In the same way that life was growing to gigantic sizes on land. the marine environment included some of the largest predators in Earth's history. There were the Liopleurodon and the Temnodontosaurus.

The breakup of the Pangaea supercontinent meant the global climate changes allowed provided the right conditions for forests to become lush and cover most of the landscape. As with the Triassic, conifers continued to dominate the flora and continued to evolve into various species. Including: Pinaceae, Podocarpaceae, Cephalotaxaceae and Taxaceae.

2. Climate

Due to the gradual breakup and drifting of Pangaea, the formerly dry and barren areas of internal regions of the supercontinent were now experiencing comfortably warm conditions.

Evidence of coral reefs, suggest the atmosphere was moist and temperate or tropical. The movements of the former Pangaea caused Africa to split from South America and Asia moved toward India. North America started to drift to the West, the Atlantic Ocean opened between two main landmasses.

Volcanic activity was triggered by the North American drift, that would gradually form the Rocky Mountains. The drifting of Pangaea still continues.

The Polar regions were devoid of ice-caps, meaning that global ocean levels were higher than today with more shallow marine environments. This facilitated the evolution of more diversity in varieties of marine creatures. With such a warm, stable climate, the numbers of different species increased greatly during the Jurassic period.

3. Life

The new lush, green forests of the Jurassic provided an endless source of food for the herbivore Sauropods such as the Brachiosaurs, Diplodocus and Apatosaurus.

These dinosaurs grew to gigantic sizes. The herbivores were the largest animals of the Jurassic.

Carnivore dinosaurs were also larger than their ancestors in the previous Triassic period. The fiercest of these were the extremely large, Allosaurus and the Ceratosaurs. The top predator would have been the Allosaurus, with a length of nine metres. Its prey would have been the large herbivores, such as the Sauropods. Flying reptiles consisted of Pterosaurs. During the later stages of the Jurassic, early birds appeared. They were the Archaeopteryx, although, the dinosaur has more in common with today's birds.

The primary vertebrates living in the oceans of the Jurassic were fish and marine reptiles. Gradually the Plesiosaurs, Pliosaurs and marine crocodiles, Ichthyosaurs reached the peak of their diversity.

Several new groups of invertebrates evolved including the Rudists, which were a reef-forming bivalve and belemnites. The ammonites were by far the most prolific, and evolved fast into different groups.

Section 4. **Cretaceous Period**

1. Cretaceous Period

The Cretaceous Period is the third geological period, of the Mesozoic era. 144 million, until 65 million years ago. The Cretaceous is the last geological period of the Mesozoic era.

The name for Cretaceous Period was coined by Belgian geologist, Jean d'Omalius d'Halloy in 1822.using strata in the Paris Basin. The Cretaceous Period derives from the Latin word, Creta, meaning, chalk, - after the chalk deposits of Southern England and Northern France, which had formed during this period.

This is the geological time that marks the height followed by demise of the dinosaur. The Cretaceous was relatively warm in most regions of Earth. Shallow seas covered much of what is now land, resulting in shallow inland seas. These oceans and seas were populated with now extinct reptiles, Ammonites and Rudists. Thick Sedimentary deposits containing oil and metal ores, copper and aluminium included, were laid down.

Mountain building continued through the Cretaceous, resulting in the formation of the Rocky Mountains and the Andes.

The Far East and Middle east were reshaped as a result of volcanic activity. Seas began to withdraw towards the end of the period. New groups of mammals and birds, also flowering plants, appeared during the period.

The Cretaceous ended with one of the most severe mass extinctions in Earth's history. This was the time when all the dinosaurs died out including the most famous, Tyrannosaurus Rex, Triceratops, Stegosaurus and the flying Pterosaurs. The birds, lizards, crocodiles, snakes and mammals. which suffered few or little extinction were exceptions at this time.

The cause of the Cretaceous mass extinction, after the discovery of Iridium in sedimentary layers, known as the K-T boundary, is attributed to a giant asteroid impact in the Mexican Yucatan peninsula. Fossil evidence is found in New Zealand, as well as North America and Denmark, of a new species of Mosasaur and Dinosaur Fauna. A single vertebrate was found to be that of an upright carnivorous land dinosaur dating back to the Cretaceous extinction event.

2. Climate

The climate of the early Cretaceous began warm and humid similar to that of the previous Jurassic Period. The Pangaea supercontinent had broken up and different continents were drifting to become the continents we see today. Once flowering plants evolved and appeared on the landscape, which in turn, contributed to an increase insect population.

The polar regions were devoid of ice caps as they had been in the Jurassic, leading to high ocean levels. In turn these created shallow coastal waters and the development of endless swamps, another ecological niche in which dinosaurs and other prehistoric life could prosper.

The late Cretaceous was marred by increased volcanic activity, which pumped extra carbon dioxide into the atmosphere, increasing global temperatures.

3. Life

The Cretaceous commenced as the previous Jurassic finished. Gigantic, slumbering herbivores roamed the landscape, taking advantage of the lush green forests. Gigantic Sauropods were still the favourite prey of the smaller ferocious carnivores.

Marine long necked reptiles still terrorised fish, ammonites and mollusks in the oceans. Pteropods and the first feathered birds dominated the skies above the changing landscapes, thanks to the continuous movements of the world's landmasses.

Dinosaurs ruled throughout the Cretaceous. Many new groups evolved during this time and many species shifted from the Jurassic. Sauropods became dominant in the southern continents and were rare in the northern continents. Herd species such as Iguanadons lived everywhere, except Antarctica.

Vast herds of Triceratops munched on cycads and other low lying plants on the northern continents. Towards the late Cretaceous, the fierce Tyrannosaurus Rex dominated the North. Along the expanding coastlines, salamanders, snakes, turtles and crocodiles thrived.

Under the immense forests, little mammals scurried from place to place.

In the oceans, modern sharks and rays became common. Sea Urchins and starfish thrived. Coral reefs grew continuously in the shallow, warm coastal waters of the continents. The first shelled plankton appeared in the oceans.

Flowering trees and plants began to dominate the land. These species thrived with the abundant numbers of bees and other numerous of insects of the Cretaceous.

According to the fossil records of the period, fern plants were also thriving. The end of the Cretaceous was the divining moment for the Pterosaurs. By this time, they had reached the height of their evolution and were beginning to wane. They were gradually being replaced by the first true birds. These bird species were evolving from previous feathered land-based dinosaurs.

Section 5. **Cretaceous Mass Extinction**

1. Evidence

A layer of iridium was found in the K-T boundary, in Alberta in the 1980s. Iridium is very rare on Earth, but is abundant in meteorites. Since the discovery, further iridium discoveries have been found in Denmark, New Zealand and North America.

The father and son team who discovered the iridium in Alberta, Luis and Walter Alvarez, suggested a huge, 'miles wide' asteroid or comet hit the Earth at the time of the Mesozoic Era.

In the Mexican Yucatan Peninsula, is a crater, partly under the ocean and worn down. This crater's creation coincides with the K-T boundary findings. NASA scientists estimate that the asteroid would have been about six to twelve miles in diameter that made the Chicxulub Crater as it is now called. The crater is 130 miles wide.

Scientists in Colorado have traced the path of that asteroid back into space. According to their calculations 160 million years ago, a collision occurred between two asteroids. A 100-mile wide Baptistina, as it is called, and a smaller asteroid out beyond the orbit of Mars, shattered the larger asteroid and sent pieces of it into the Solar System 95 million years later. These pieces crashed into Earth, 65 million years ago, causing 70 percent of plant and animal life on Earth to perish. This coincides with the end of the Mesozoic era.

There are a number of crater sites around the world that date back to the Mesozoic era. The crater in Yucatan, Mexico, is the most likely site of the asteroid strike that triggered the mass extinction. This site was accidentally discovered in 1991, by geologists, drilling for oil.

2. Effects on Earth

It is hard to imagine the effect that the impact such an asteroid event would have on the planet world, especially as it affected life. One of the effects or consequences of such an impact would be the largest mega tsunami's in Earth's history - reaching thousands of metres high. Colossal shock waves would have triggered global earthquakes and volcanic eruptions.

Massive dust clouds, which would block sunlight and inhibit photosynthesis for a few years and cause the extinction of plants. Phytoplankton and organisms dependent on them. These would include predatory animals and herbivores.

Small creatures, whose food chains were based on organic material, might have had a reasonable chance for survival. It is estimated that sulphuric acid aerosols, were injected into the stratosphere., leading to a 10 - 20 percent reduction in the sun's rays reaching the surface of the Earth. It would take about ten years for those aerosols to dissipate.

As incendiary fragments fell back to Earth. Global firestorms would have ignited. Analysts suggest the oxygen content of the atmosphere was very high, maybe 30-35 percent during the Cretaceous period. This high oxygen level would have supported intense combustion.

The level of atmospheric plummeted in the early Tertiary Period. If widespread fires occurred, they would have increased the carbon dioxide content of the atmosphere and caused a temporary greenhouse effect. Once the dust cloud settled. This would have exterminated the most vulnerable survivors of the long winter. The impact might also have produced acid rain.

The survival of animals vulnerable to acid rain effects, such as frogs, indicates that this was not a major contributor to extinction.

CHAPTER SIX

Age Of Mammals

Section 1. **Cenozoic Era**

1, The Cenozoic Era's meaning -'recent life'. The Era began in the wake of the Cretaceous extinction event, that saw the demise of the last non-avian dinosaurs, as well as other unique marine flora and fauna at the end of the Mesozoic era.

The Cenozoic is also known as the, 'Age of Mammals', because the extinction, of the non-avian dinosaurs allowed a great diversification among them and domination of the Earth. This era era continues to the present time.

The Cenozoic era began 65 million years ago and includes three periods in the history of the Earth and evolution known as the Paleogene, Neogene and Quaternary.

2, Climate

The supercontinents of Gondwana have broken away and the landmasses have been drifting into their current positions. More land is now accessible to the oceans.

The climate is cooler now than the previous Cretaceous period as the movement of the landmasses assist in creating oceanic currents that now, moderate the global temperatures.

Early in the Cenozoic era, two million years ago, ice caps started forming at the poles. Earth's climate had become cold enough to support large ice sheets at both Poles.

During the most recent 2.6 million years of Earth's history, glaciers advanced from the Poles followed by a retreat, their action carving and moulding the land with each cycle. Sea levels fell and rose with each period of freezing and thawing.

3. Life

The Cenozoic era is the time in which whales dominated the oceans sharing with porpoises, fish and octopi. The forests became lush and the habitat of elephants, sabre-toothed cats, giant rhinos, lions, horses and deer. Small mouse-like mammalian creatures diversified and grew in size. The skies became filled with birds and bats.

The Paleogene period that occurred about 40 million years ago, at the beginning of the Cenozoic era, was the time when mammals evolved from the small creatures of the Cretaceous. Some mammals evolved into large forms that could dominate the land. Others adapted and thrived, living in marine, and airborne environments. Other species took to the trees and became primates, the group to which humans belong.

Birds underwent considerable evolutionary change becoming roughly like their modern varieties. Most other life forms remained relatively unchanged, by comparison with birds and mammals.

During this period, tropical plants became restricted to equatorial regions. Deciduous plants became more common as they adapted for survival through the now seasonal climate. One of the most notable developments of flora during this period was the arrival of the first grass species. This new plant type expanded and formed the ecological environments known today as savannas and prairies. These grasslands, owing to their ability to survive in drier climates, began to replace typical forests in many regions of the world.

The Neogene Period was about 24 million years ago. Mammals and birds continued as the dominant vertebrates, adopting various forms as they adapted to various habitats. The first hominids ancestors of humans appeared in Africa and spread to Eurasia. Tropical plant species gave way to deciduous plants and grasslands continued to replace many forests.

As grasses diversified into many varieties, herbivorous mammals evolved alongside them. Many modern varieties of grazing animals such as horses, sheep, antelope and bison, also evolved.

The Quaternary period, began 1.8 million years ago is known as 'the Age Of Humans'. The Quaternary period continues today. Humans evolved in Africa 190 thousand years ago, dispersing globally, while continuing to evolve.

Present day mammals, flowering plants and insects dominated the land. During only 10,000 years, (a blink of an eye in geological and evolutionary time) humanity has spread over all areas of the globe, altering the face of the Earth. Starting with farms, expanded into villages then cities, humanity has destroyed some plants, habitats and the animals who occupy them and domesticated others.

Humans have become the dominant life form, more fearsome than most terrible dinosaurs.

4. Continents

The Cenozoic era, geographically is the era when the continents moved into the position they hold today. Australia and New Guinea had split from Gondwana during the early Cretaceous, drifting north until eventually colliding with Southeast Asia. Antarctica moved in to its current position over the South Pole. The Atlantic Ocean widened, then later in the era, South America became attached to North America. India collided with Asia about 50 million years ago. Arabia collided with Eurasia, closing the Tethys Ocean around 30 million years ago.

5. The Advance Of Humanity

Throughout more than 90 percent of its history, homo sapiens lived in small bands as nomadic hunter gatherers. Communication became important and language eventually became more complex. As a result, the ability to remember and communicate information developed importance for learning. A new replicator known as the "Meme" evolved enabling the exchange of ideas and their passage down through generations. Cultural evolution quickly outpaced biological evolution.

The development of agriculture about 10,000 years ago, in the Middle East, gave humans the opportunity to become farmers. Agriculture spread to neighbouring areas then expanded independently in other areas.

Whilst not all societies abandoned their nomadic life, those who did adopt it, expanded their societies with relative stability and productivity.

Agriculture had a major effect on civilization. As societies grew and were able to sustain this growth, civilisations quickly arose, settling in ancient Egypt, around the Indus River Valley and in China.

More complex societies arose through the invention of writing and record keeping. Libraries served as a storehouse of knowledge and increased the transmission of cultural information. Education drove the pursuit of knowledge and wisdom. New civilisations arose and traded with one another and fought for territory and resources.

Around 70,000 years ago there were empires in the Middle East, Iran, India, China, and Greece. Empires expanded, only to decline or be driven back later. Societies continued to grow and spread globally with new discoveries and colonisation of new lands at times, resulting in conflict.

6. Technological Advances

Technological advancement and change has continued at increased speed since the 1940s, especially in science. This has resulted in nuclear weapons, computers, nano technology, and genetic engineering, along with advancements in communication and transport technology.

In 1957, the Soviet Union launched the first artificial satellite into Earth's orbit, heralding the beginning of the space race. The World Wide Web was developed in the 1990s creating the new storehouse for knowledge.

Section 2. **Paleogene Period**

1. Paleogene Period

is the first geological period, of the Cenozoic era, lasting from 65 million until 23 million years ago.

The Paleogene Period, is most noted as the period in time when the mammals diversified and grew from the small creatures of the previous, Cretaceous, period. At the beginning of the Paleogene, dinosaurs, pterosaurs and giant marine reptiles, were noticeably absent from the face of the Earth.

The continents continued their drift, filling voids on the planet, gradually becoming recognisably the continents that we see today. Along with the various oceans and oceanic currents, that control, present day temperatures worldwide. Europe finally split from North America, and Australia split from Antarctica.

As the climate significantly cooled and dried, sea levels continued to drop, from Cretaceous levels. The end of the Paleogene period was marked with a significant period of global change during the Cenozoic. The Paleogene, Eocene thermal maximum led to the extinction of numerous deep-sea species after the thermal maximum disturbed oceanic and atmospheric circulation.

2. Climate

The climate of the Paleogene period was significantly cooler than the previous Cretaceous period. This obviously had an effect on the plant life that had diversified so well during the tropical and humid climatic conditions of the Cretaceous. Instead of the tropical plants, land plants became more deciduous. The first grass also appeared during the Paleogene.

Continents continued their drift towards their current positions.

- India was in the process of colliding with Asia, and forming the Himalayas.

- The Atlantic ocean continued to widen, forcing North America further away from Europe.

- Africa was inching closer to Europe and forming the Mediterranean sea. South America was moving closer to North America.

- Australia had broken away from Antarctica and was moving closer to Southeast Asia.

- The formation of the Antarctic circumpolar current significantly cooled the oceanic water temperatures and continues to do so.

3. Life

Modern sharks evolved to fill the void from the massive mosasaurs and plesiosaurs of the Cretaceous oceans. Sharks shared the space with various forms of fish, squid and soft bodied cephalopods that had evolved to replace their shelled relatives. Bivalves and sea snails lurked on the ocean floors. New types of sea urchins were also present in the oceans, replacing their ancestors of the Cretaceous.

The most notable development for the world's oceans, however, was the arrival of whales. These huge marine animals evolved from land mammals that had taken to the seas. Turtles, crocodiles, snakes and lizards had survived the mass extinction that marked the end of the Cretaceous Period and were able to enjoy and diversify in the new climatic conditions of the Paleogene period.

In the skies, birds that had maintained their species from the early ancestors began to diversify and flourish in the skies.

None of these changes and diversification compared to that of the mammals. Compared to the little mouse like creatures of the previous period, primates, horses, bats, pigs, cats and dogs had evolved towards the end of the Paleogene Period.

As the climate cooled during this period, woodlands developed concurrently with grasslands in the northern hemisphere. These features supported herds of grazing mammals.

The climatic cooling of the Paleogene Period affected plant life. Tropical plants were decreased as they be- came restricted to equatorial areas. Deciduous trees were able to survive the temperature variations now being experienced on Earth. With variable seasonal changes the drier conditions, formed new ecological environments. From forests, to woodlands and the appearance of grass species in savannas and prairies, as grasses could survive and diversify in drier conditions, more successfully than Forests.

Section 3. **Neogene Period**

1. The Neogene Period,

Is the second geological period, of the Cenozoic era, 23 million years ago to the present.

The Neogene also includes the traditional period, Quaternary period which is, modern times. Not surprisingly, during the early, Neogene period, planet Earth closely resembled the Earth that we now know. The continental landmasses were situated close to their present day positions.

Appearances can be deceiving. At the beginning of the Neogene, continents continued to collide with each other, forcing mountains to rise and sea levels to fall. Species were forced to adapt as sea levels dropped.

India continued on its collision course with Asia continuing the rise of the Himalayan ranges.

Italy collided with Europe, forcing the uprising of the Pyrenees. The high Mountains caused changes to air currents and contributed to the cooler climate.

Arctic ice caps grew thicker, locking huge quantities of oceanic waters. Snow fell and ice formed on the high mountain peaks.

Land bridges were exposed as sea levels plummeted uncovering land between continents such as Africa and Eurasia, Eurasia and North America. This enabled species which had evolved in isolation to spread and further diversify.

Grasslands formed in the drier conditions over much land previously occupied with forest, forcing other species to adapt or die.

Horses evolved stronger and larger, bison, giraffes, sheep and camels, that had developed compartmental stomachs to digest a diet of grass, flourished. Many grazers became fleet footed and formed herds against the predators that had also been forced to adapt.

2, Climate

The global climate during the Neogene continued to cool from the previous Paleogene period and became seasonal and drier. Ice caps began to grow thicker in the Polar regions. Snow was falling in mountainous areas. By the end of the Period, the first glaciations of the current ice age had begun.

Movement and rearrangment of the Earth's continents greatly affected oceans currents and thereby greatly changing the global climate. Oxygen levels were settling to modern levels of 21 percent, compared to the Permian mass extinction when they rose dramatically and peaked at 35 percent.

Landmasses were rising due to volcanic activity. Iceland was in the process of rising. New Zealand contin-

ued its rise, which had begun during the Triassic period. All mountain ranges formed through the rear-
rangement of landmasses, including the Alps, Andes,
Appalachians, Cascades, Rockies and Himalayas.

3, Life

Marine and land based species were relatively similar
to the various species that exist today, with a few exceptions. Mammals and Birds continue to dominate
both the Ocean environments and land environments.

A large brown algae, Kelp, appeared in the oceans.
Locking onto shallow water corals and rock, establish-
ing new habitats for other species. Such as Otters as
well as a large variety of small fish species. Again,
sharks dominated the seas. The largest shark of all, the
Megalodon, dominated among them all. These species
measured a gigantic, 15 metres in length.

On land, Woolly Mammoths and Saber toothed Cats
appeared in Africa and Asia. Ape species diversified.
Our earliest ancestors, the first Hominids, split from
our closest relative. Adapted their stance by standing
on two feet. Appeared in Africa and slowly spread into
Eurasia. These new species were poised to alter the
planet, unlike any other species in the history of Life
On Earth.

CHAPTER SEVEN

Time Of Humans

Section 1. **Quaternary Period**

1, Today

T oday, in the geological time scale, life on Earth is still in the Quaternary Period of the Cenozoic era which will last another two million years.

Humans have colonised most areas of the landmasses on Earth.

Land movements have been to the minimal, partly due to the short duration. So far of the Quaternary Period. land movement has been less than 100 kilometres.

Few major animals have evolved, again because of the short, in geologic terms duration of the period. There have however been a few extinctions. Sabre toothed cats, mammoths, mastodons and glyptodonts are among the few species that have become extinct during the short duration. Man's continuing quest to colonise and develop lands and hunting threaten to make further flora, and fauna species extinct. Seventeen thousand animal species are at risk of extinction, including 21 percent of mammal species, 12 percent of birds, 28 percent of reptiles, 30 percent of amphibians, 35 percent of invertebrates,37 percent of freshwater fish and 70 percent of plants.

2, Climate

Since the beginning of the Cenozoic era, Earth's climate has been going through a period of long term cooling, due to the continued tectonic activity, volcanic activity and drifting of landmasses, changing the face of Earth together with the formation of oceanic currents regulating Earth's temperatures and atmosphere.

The climate cooled significantly due to the appearance of the Antarctic circum-polar current, which brought cool deep Antarctic water to the surface; the formation of Drake Passage, when South America fully detached from Antarctica. The cooling trend continued with relatively short warmer periods when South America became attached to North America, creating the Isthmus of Panama. The Arctic region cooled due to the strengthening of the Humboldt and Gulf Stream currents.

Today, Earth receives and absorbs more heat in the tropics than at the poles. Oceanic currents distribute this heat in uniform temperatures towards polar areas. As you have read in this book. carbon dioxide levels, in comparison with oxygen levels can, and certainly do play an important role in regulation of the Earth's climatic conditions. Too low levels of CO^2 and too high levels of oxygen have, in Earths history, played a major contributing factor on Snowball Earth events. Too high and low levels of oxygen have also played a major contributing factor to Snowball Earth events and glaciation events. Today, the Earth is facing another climatic rise in carbon dioxide. Earth's climate is changing due to this dramatic increase in CO^2 compared to the oxygen levels, present in Earths atmosphere.

3, Life

Over the centuries leading up to the mid 20th century , the human population has fluctuated due to both natural causes and human causes. Famines, genocides, epidemics such as plagues in Europe and Asia, and conflicts. Natural causes were probably due to an unprecedented number of volcanic eruptions.

The middle ages experienced a global warming period, causing changes in the ocean circulation and resulting in the Little Ice Age, between 1550 and 1850. This event was not a true ice age, but global temperatures decreased.

The most recent study found that an especially massive tropical volcanic eruption in 1258, followed by three smaller eruptions in 1268, 1275, and 1284 that did not allow the climate to recover, caused the initial cooling. The 1452 to 1453 eruption of Kuwae in Vanuatu triggered a second phase of cooling.

The beginning of the 20th Century, saw two major conflicts: World Wars 1 and 2 between 1914 and 1918 and from 1939 to 1945, resulting in over 90 million casualties between both conflicts.

Since the beginning of the 21st Century, the Earths population has exceeded 7 billion humans. The 20th Century saw the strongest growth figures from the 1950s, witnessing its highest rate in the 1980s of 138 million births per year. Earths population has seen a steady increase from 370 million at the end of the great famine and Black Death in 1350.

In response to the new climate of the Quaternary period, a wave of new plant species emerged, despite the development of a much less favourable climate for species adapted to moist conditions. Most tertiary species that have been tracked through the fossil record did not disappear.

A large number of ancient tertiary species in Mediterranean climate ecosystems appear to have been preserved by the facilitating, nurse effects of modern species.

Conserving ecological traits over evolutionary time scales, flowering seed bearing plants spread rapidly. Herbaceous plants, pine trees, grape vines, oaks and spruces, evolved as they can better handle changing seasons. Insects and plants evolved together. The first nectar eating birds and bats appeared. Plants that were fertilised by wind gave way to insect fertilising plants. Some grasses and trees reverted to wind fertilisation.

4, Atmosphere

Earth's atmosphere is a layer of gases surrounding the planet, which is retained by Earth's gravity. The atmosphere protects life on Earth by absorbing solar radiation and heating the surface, then releasing ultraviolet radiation that heats the air through heat retention, reducing heat extremes between day and night.

Atmospheric stratification divides the distinctive layers, with specific characteristics such as temperature or composition. The atmosphere becomes thinner in higher altitudes, with no specific boundary with space. An altitude of 120 kilometres is where atmospheric effects become noticeable during spacecraft re-entry.

The major gases of the atmosphere are: nitrogen, oxygen and argon. The remaining gases are trace gases or greenhouse gases, water vapour, carbon dioxide, methane, nitrous oxide and ozone, ozone being the top layer in the stratosphere. Other substances may be present. Including: dust, pollen and spores and sea spray.

Volcanic ash and industrial pollutants may also be present such as: chlorine, fluorine, mercury and sulphur dioxide.

5, Evolution Of Earth's Atmosphere

Until a steady state was established outgassing of the Earth, hydrogen and helium were stripped away by solar winds, early in the history of the planet.

The first atmosphere based on today's volcanic evidence, would have contained 60 percent hydrogen and 20 percent oxygen (though this oxygen would have been as water vapour), 10 percent carbon dioxide. 5 -7 percent hydrogen sulphide, inert gases along with smaller amounts of carbon monoxide, methane and free hydrogen.

Major rainfalls precipitated the build-up of vast oceans, enriching the atmosphere with carbon dioxide then later nitrogen. A large amount of emissions were dissolved in water and built up carbonate sediments. The second atmosphere occurred about 3.4 billion years ago. Nitrogen was a major component of the stable atmosphere. Compared to today, the sun's illumination was 30 percent lower, as life was developing during the Archaean eon. The oxygen content was increasing due to Stroma-tolites on Earth's surface 2.4 billion years ago.

The third atmosphere is that with which we are familiar today. Plate tectonics were continually rearranging continents and shaping long, term climate evolution. Free oxygen was not available until about 1.7 billion years ago, which signified a move from a shifting atmosphere to an oxidising atmosphere. Carbon dioxide levels fluctuated, until it reached a steady 15 percent.

Currently greenhouse gases are increasing, causing global climate change and heating the atmosphere.

Section 2. **Human Legacy**

1. Future Predictions

Countless times, someone has predicted the future and events for the future of Earth that have proved baseless. Towards the end of the 20th century, some predictions were centred, around the change from the 20th to 21st centuries, with computer technology and the "Y2K Bug"; predicting that modern computer technology would identify a series of 0's in dating as the end of a computer programme. It was believed that this would result in important infrastructure closing down, creating chaos throughout the world. More recently surrounding the Mayan calendar, with predictions of a catastrophic end to time and all life on Earth, in 2012. Which, obviously did not come to fruition.

These predictions have absolutely no scientific basis so should be dismissed and also any source claiming they hold any dire predictions for Earth and life's future, whose followers evangelize these predictions that have absolutely no scientific basis. They are scaremongering and belong securely in the realms of fantasy.

As mentioned in Chapter One, to be recognised as fact, any hypothesis or notion must be able to be observed and tested numerous times and able to be tested against historical evidence. It must be seen to be believed, otherwise it is pure assumption. In this section, I will produce evidence; evidence that has been tested and observed numerous times, and just as numerously, proven to be true, thus. This evidence is Fact.

2. Fossil Fuels

Humans are dependent on the use of fossil fuels and over recent times have allowed themselves to be dependent on fuels that have taken 300-600 million years to develop, right under their feet.

It is a popular misconception that fossil fuels are formed from dead dinosaurs. This misconception may be due to experts explaining the process that leads to

the formation of fossil fuels and including the term,
'Prehistoric times.'

Most people refer to prehistoric, as the precise time dinosaurs dominated the Earth. The dead life forms that
eventually formed fossil fuels were laid down millions
of years before the Mesozoic era, when dinosaur
evolved and dominated the Earth, and would have included the very first living organisms on Earth before
and after life diversified from the sea to land. These
organisms, animals and plants when they died, would
have been covered by multiple layers of mud, rock and
sand. As they decomposed, over the years, layers built
up to hundreds of metres. Those dead animals and
plants continued to decompose and formed organic material which then formed different types of fossil fuels.

For example, coal, natural gas and oil. Natural gas and
oil were formed from the intense pressure underground
during the decomposition process where a bacterium
was introduced along with this pressure and bacteria.
The compression "cooked" the organic matter under
the layers of silt. Oil first formed in some deeper, hotter
regions underground. This cooking process continued
and natural gas was formed. Over time, some of this oil
and natural gas began migrating upward through the
Earth's crust; until they ran into harder rock called, cap
rocks, dense enough to prevent them from migrating to
the surface.

It is from under these cap rocks that most oil and natural gas is found today. The same forces formed coal.
Coal is made from dead plants, ferns, trees and other
plants left behind in swamps and bogs, containing large

amounts of sulphur, when the seas retreated. The sulphur reacted with the plant material and formed coal. Some coal however was formed in swamps and bogs that didn't contain sulphur. The pressure and heat from decomposition after the wetlands dried up or retreated contributed to the coals' formation.

Fossil fuels produce carbon dioxide as a by-product, when burned. Human dependence on fossil fuels is disturbing, as the use of these fuels, increases the Earth's, CO_2 levels. Carbon dioxide is water-soluble. Water and especially the world's oceans, absorb and dissolve large amounts of atmospheric carbon dioxide. The CO_2 dissolves slowly falling to the oceans' floor. Oceans are like a sponge, but like any sponge, it can only absorb so much without creating major problems, as CO_2 reacts with water and creates carbonic acid. The oceans thus become increasingly more acidic.

Natural forces also produce CO_2, for example volcanic eruptions. Volcanic eruptions are the Earth's atmospheric regulator in the natural world. Because carbon dioxide is dissolved in the oceans, falling to the floor as biomass and as the levels of carbon dioxide in the atmosphere is dissipated due to this absorption, volcanic eruptions boost the atmospheric CO_2 allowing the natural process to continue. Life on Earth also depends on levels of atmospheric CO_2 for photosynthesis. If it weren't for volcanic eruptions, life may not be possible on Earth.

In 2011, Terrance Gerlach, a scientist from the U.S. Geological survey. Calculated on average, humans emit more CO_2 in 3-5 days than volcanoes do globally in a year. Gerlach suggests human induced emissions may exceed the output of one or more super eruptions, the largest being the Mount Toba eruption in Indonesia, 74,000 thousand years ago. Gerlach estimates human induced emissions are about 35 million tons per year, which is 100-300, times the emissions from volcanoes.

Volcanic ash is thicker and heavier than CO^2, which is a gas. The effects on Earth's climate, is considerably shorter in duration, as the volcanic ash will fall back to the Earth's surface within a short time, one year, to a few years depending on the weight of the ash and the severity of the eruption.

Gas is lighter than ash, so will remain in the atmosphere indefinitely. CO^2 is a greenhouse gas that traps heat in the atmosphere. Without it and other greenhouse gases, Earth would be a frozen world.

Now with our dependence on fossil fuels, there is about 30 percent more CO^2 in the air than there was about 150 years ago, and Earth's climate is changing. Ice core samples show us that there is now more CO^2 in the atmosphere than there has been in the last 420-thousand years, when the overall temperatures on Earth were markedly higher than today. The continued dependence on fossil fuels is increasing the CO^2 emissions beyond manageable levels.

3.   Fossil Fuel Dependence

More than 30 years ago, our dependence on fossil fuels took up about 75 percent of our energy source. Today's estimates put it at 90 percent representing a huge increase. Considering that about a hundred years ago, fossil fuels were practically unheard of, today, the burning of fossil fuels produces about 21.3 billion tons of CO_2 per year. It is estimated the natural processes that absorb CO_2, can only absorb half that amount. This would account for about 10.6 billion tons of CO_2 being released into the atmosphere every year, and causing Earth's average surface temperature to rise accordingly.

The use of fossil fuels has become an important aspect of modern life. Its uses are wide and varied. Oil is used in most modern products. Most plastic products contain oil, ranging from soft drink bottles, milk bottles, detergent bottles to shopping bags, etc . Tar and bitumen used in building roads are oil products. Rubber, for vehicle tyres use oil. Cosmetic products, such as: perfumes, lipstick, hand lotions, shampoo, toothpaste and deodorants etc use oil and petroleum products. And of course the power source for cars, trucks, trains, airplanes and ships use oil and petroleum based fuels.

In the generation of electricity, coal is the fuel used worldwide in the greatest quantities for the generation of electricity. Coal is also used for steel production and the manufacture of cement, as well as for heating. Global CO_2 emissions from coal account for slightly more than that from, petroleum and double the amount from natural gas.

Natural gas consists of methane, ethane and small amounts of CO_2, and is used primarily for heating, cooking, electricity generation and producing fertilisers for agricultural applications. When burned, natural gas produces large amounts of CO^2. Global estimated usage of Fossil fuels:

- Oil consumption - 86.6 million barrels per day,
- Petroleum consumption - 87 million barrels per day,
- Natural Gas consumption - 62,920,033 cubic metres per day,
- Coal consumption - 18,476,000 short tons per day.

4. Some Misconceptions

There are many misconceptions around Global Climate Change, Personally I feel there may be many reasons for these along with the number of skeptics, who either do not understand the scientific findings confirming global climate change or simply prefer not to believe them.

The reasons can be as varied as from looking out a window and not seeing any changes and so coming to the conclusion that global climates are not changing or preferring to believe another source providing information that they personally, want to believe. In other words, ignorance of the world around them.

Misconceptions are varied and range from confusion between global climate change and the ozone layer. The ozone layer has absolutely nothing to do with global climate change. The hole in the ozone layer is caused by CFC's, not CO^2 emissions.

There is a suggestion that 1934 was the hottest year on record. The fact is 1934, was the hottest year on record, but only in the US. A heat wave in the US does not account for the rest of the world!

The United States National Oceanic and Atmospheric Administration (NOAA) when comparing their weather records since 1895 declared July of 2012 the hottest July on record, with average temperatures being 25.3 degrees Celsius. This was significantly higher than the highest temperature in 1934. NOAA also says the temperatures for July have been steadily increasing since 2006.

Fluctuation in weather pattern may cause slightly lower temperatures, but on average, temperatures are continuing to rise, this average rise is likely to continue for decades to come.

There are some claims that it was a cold summer, local climate does not account for the global climate.

Other misconceptions are around Arctic ice. There are claims that ice sheets are expanding. Evidence along with satellite data confirms that Arctic ice sheets are retreating rapidly, along with glaciers.

There are other claims that the climate isn't warming because of larger than normal snowfalls, global climate warming does cause more water vapour, which causes heavier precipitation or rain and heavier snow falls.

5. Deforestation

A major natural method for recycling is forestry, through photosynthesis. Forests turn CO^2 into oxygen. Forests still cover about 30 percent of the Earth's landmass, as part of the global carbon cycle. Large areas about the size of Panama are cleared each year. Forests are cleared for many reasons, mainly for agriculture, for grazing livestock or crops. Other reasons are logging, for world supply of paper and paper products and urban growth of cities and towns.

A major misconception of deforestation however is that the logging of forests is for building timbers. These operations usually require the forests to be replanted for the next generation of building materials. So technically, cannot be called or termed, 'deforestation.'

Thirteen million hectares of land are cleared each year by deforestation. contributing 20 percent of global CO^2 emissions. This equates to as much as cars, trucks, trains, airplanes and boats combined.

Deforestation is a major contributor to global climate change, as forest floors are moist, assisting in the water cycle, contributing vapour into the atmosphere. Without the protection of forest cover this land dries out fast and can quickly become barren.

Over recent years, the rate of deforestation has shown signs of decreasing, but the rate is still alarmingly high. In the 1990s, 16 million hectares were cleared annually.

6, Global Warming

Global climate change does not refer to regional or local climate conditions. As the name or term suggests, it is referring to the global climate, which is created by weather patterns, oceanic currents and winds worldwide, and refers to the average climatic conditions. It is a significant and lasting change in the statistical distribution of weather patterns over periods ranging from decades to millions of years.

As you read in the first section of this chapter, the Earth's atmosphere consists of greenhouse gases, primarily water vapour, and smaller amounts of CO_2, methane and nitrous oxide. These gases act as a thermal blanket for the Earth, absorbing heat and warming the surface to a life supporting average of 15 degrees Celsius or 59 degree Fahrenheit.

Life on Earth depends on energy from the sun. Light from the sun is filtered through the ozone layer, when about half the amount of light passes through to the Earth's surface, heat is radiated up as infra red heat. About 90 percent of the infra red heat is absorbed by the greenhouse gases in the atmosphere and reflected back to the Earths surface.

Foregoing chapters explain the changes to Earth's climate, has been through during the entire history of the Earth.

There have been seven cycles of glacial advance and retreat in the last 650 thousand years. The last ice age ended abruptly 7,000 years ago marking the beginning of modern day climate and the human era.

The Earth's orbit is elliptical. An elliptical orbit allows slight variations in the orbit with the sun, which changes the amount of solar energy the Earth receives. This is the reason for those changes to Earth's climate.

Technological advances, in particular artificial satellites, have allowed scientists to see what is happening with Earth's climate over recent years. Studying the collected data indicates that Earth's climate is changing globally, and very abruptly.

Throughout Earth's history, such changes have taken thousands of years. These modern changes are occurring within decades from the amount of human induced CO_2 emissions. These changes include:

- Global Temperature Warming: with most of the warming occurring since the 1970s and the greater amount of this warming since 1981. The warmest years being within the first decade of the 21st century. This warming trend is believed to continue.

- Rising Ocean Levels: The last century witnessed a sea level rise of 17 centimetres. The first decade of the 21st century's sea level rise is believed to double last century's level.

- Shrinking Ice Sheets:According to NASA. the ice sheets of Antarctica and Greenland have decreased in mass, Antarctica losing 150 cubic kilometres of ice sheet, Greenland losing 150 - 250 kilometres of ice sheet within three years.

- Warming Oceans: The top 700 metres of ocean surface heating by -17.61 degrees Celsius or 0.302 Degrees Fahrenheit since 1969.

- Decreasing Arctic Sea Ice:Over the last 7 decades, Arctic sea ice has declined in both thickness and extent. rapidly. Satellite data tells us that Arctic sea ice is now declining at a rate of 11.5 percent, per decade.

- Glacial Retreat: Almost all glaciers around the world are retreating.

- Extreme Weather Events: The number of extreme weather events are increasing globally. Including: snowfalls, rainfalls, droughts, cyclones and storms. While the record number of low temperatures have been decreasing globally.

- Ocean Acidification: The acidity of surface waters in the oceans had increased by 30 percent since the beginning of the industrial revolution, in 1850. The amount of CO_2 absorbed by the upper layer of the oceans is increasing by about two billion tons per year. Earth's climate record suggests the average temperature of the planet has risen by just under one degree Celsius or one degree Fahrenheit. This may not sound much, but. Over Earth's history, such average temperature rises or decreases have taken thousands of years to occur. Such a rise is an unusual event in Earth's history, as global average temperature are stable over long periods of time.

Such small changes in temperature correspond to enormous changes in the environment. During the last ice age, the average global temperatures were five to nine degrees cooler than today.

The scientific community is confident the global temperature average will continue to rise over coming decades, together with the rate of human induced carbon dioxide emissions. Also there is growing concern for more severe and frequent global weather events - more droughts, heat waves, flooding, hurricanes and cyclones.

CHAPTER EIGHT

Conclusion

W hat is the direction for Life On Earth? Since the 1950s and as late as the 1970s, speculation has been whether the Earth is heading into another ice age, with the increasing CO_2 levels from human activities and their dependence on fossil fuels.

This speculation is now gaining traction from the scientific community. The Earth has existed since its formation 4.6 billion years ago. Life began with primitive cell organisms 3.5 billion years ago, until oxygen enabled more sophisticated multi celled organisms to evolve through respiration and later, photosynthesis. These two evolutionary advances were great leaps forward for life.

The process of evolution conquered all Earth and nature could throw at it over the eons. All modern life on Earth evolved from those primitive organisms. They were our common ancestors.

Life survived through the turbulent history of the planet: through asteroid impacts, extreme hot climates and extreme cold climates. Through snowball Earth events, ice ages, extreme plate tectonic activity and volcanic activity, supercontinent formations and separations and mass extinctions.

At this point in Earth's history, our planet is half way through a glacial cycle. As you have read, the Earth's orbit is elliptical. Every twenty to twenty five thousand years, the Earth's elliptical orbit increases, pushing Earth further from our Sun and plunging our planet into an ice age. These ice ages last on average one to five million years. At this present time, the Earth is in an interglacial period. Deducing from scientific observation, Earth is not due for another glacial period for another ten to eleven thousand years.

Speculation is growing that humanity's dependence on fossil fuels and the increasing levels of CO_2 could plunge the Earth into another glacial period or Snowball Earth, much sooner unless humans intervene with their use of fossil fuels.

Should this scenario occur, life may have a hard job surviving. Since life first began on Earth evolution has enabled life to adapt over long periods of time. Those evolutionary advances were not over short periods of time.

In Earth's history, large amounts of CO_2 compared to low levels of oxygen, have plunged it into Snowball events lasting millions of years. One fact is certain, such glacial period will last for one to five million years.

Through this period of the geological time scale, Earth will survive. Earth will emerge from another glacial period, no matter how severe it is. Some kind of life form will also emerge from this period and enjoy the pristine climatic conditions to be found as the planet emerges into the next period in the geologic history of life on Earth.

The evolutionary process will continue. Another form of life will develop, over another period of millions of years.

Life as we know it, along with humanity, wont have time to adapt to a sudden glacial event through evolution.

Life as we know it, will be long gone.

Appreciation

I would personally like to thank you for purchasing and reading this book. I enjoyed writing **A History Of Life On Earth**. I hope it was enjoyable for you to read.

Bruce Alpine.

For more Titles available from Bruce Alpine. Visit the Website:

https://brucealpine.com

Contact The Author:

bruce-a@brucealpine.com

Index

A History Of Life On Earth

Bruce Alpine.

ePub ISBN: 978-1-301-20346-8
Print ISBN: 978-1-493-53927-7